CULTURE AND COUNTERCULTURE IN MOROCCAN POLITICS

CULTURE AND COUNTERCULTURE IN MOROCCAN POLITICS

John P. Entelis

University Press of America, Inc.
Lanham • New York • London

Copyright © 1996 by
University Press of America,® Inc.
4720 Boston Way
Lanham, Maryland 20706

3 Henrietta Street
London, WC2E 8LU England

Originally published 1989 by Westview Press

Library of Congress Cataloging-in-Publication Data

Entelis, John P. (John Pierre).
Culture and counterculture in Moroccan politics / John P. Entelis.
p.   cm.
Originally published: Boulder : Westview Press, 1989.
Includes bibliographical references and index.
1. Morocco--Civilization--20th century. 2. Morocco--Politics and
government. 3. Politics and culture--Morocco. I. Title.
DT325.5.E58   1996   964 --dc20   96-23036   CIP

ISBN 0-7618-0392-0 (pbk: alk. ppr.)

∞™ The paper used in this publication meets the minimum
requirements of American National Standard for information
Sciences—Permanence of Paper for Printed Library Materials,
ANSI Z39.48—1984

To my lovely daughters,
DOMINIQUE and JOËLLE,
with love and admiration

Contents

Preface to the 1996 Edition

It has been nearly ten years since this book was completed. Yet, although Morocco has undergone several noticeable changes in its political economy and still others in its political structures, the country's political culture remains centered around core beliefs in Moroccanism, Islamism, and Arabism--otherwise known as the Muslim consensus. This consensus has enabled the increasingly physically feeble yet politically astute King Hassan II to navigate his modestly endowed country through troubled political and economic waters. But the challenges which have confronted his regime these last three decades remain as acute as ever--rural poverty, urban blight, economic uncertainty, political disillusionment, Islamic revivalism, bureaucratic corruption, and regional instability.

The Western Sahara conflict continues to fester, while intensified ties to Europe have forced a major restructuring of an already precarious agriculturally-based economy that is always at the mercy of unpredictable cycles of drought and rainfall. Global pressures for domestic restructuring have seen a dramatic shift in Morocco's economic orientation as private ownership and foreign investment have increasingly replaced money-losing state-run enterprises. The king has been in the forefront of this effort, hosting in Marrakesh the 1994 final meeting of the Uruguay Round in which the GATT (General Agreement on Tariffs and Trade) gave way to the new and permanent World Trade Organization. Yet there are real dangers that rapid shifts in economic priorities will hurt the poor causing popular unrest and social upheaval as were the cases with the Fez riots of December 1990, the 1991 disturbances, and, less violently, in 1995, when nation-wide strikes nearly paralyzed the country.

Politically, the regime has been as adept as ever in promoting political liberalization without allowing substantive political democracy to take hold. A revised constitution was approved overwhelmingly by plebiscite in 1992 as prelude to a new round of long-delayed national elections. The parliamentary elections held in June (direct) and October (indirect) 1993 saw a pro-government majority achieve its predictable victory. Despite claims by critics that the process was manipulated if not predetermined, the country's overall political environment remains relatively liberal by Arab world standards. Even the challenges of Islamic revivalism and unemployed youth have not forced the kind of national crackdown once considered routine for Hassan's Morocco. Indeed, in early 1996, the king felt secure enough in his political standing to release from house arrest Abdessalem Yassin, the venerable Islamic activist who had been sequestered in his Salé home since late 1989. This gesture reflects a broader process of political liberalization over the last several years that has involved the release of virtually all of the country's political prisoners. To be sure, European criticism of Moroccan human rights abuses focused unflattering attention on Rabat at a time when it was seeking a favorable hearing in Brussels for associative status in the European Union. In combination, internal and external pressures have forced an opening up consistent with the king's policy of incremental democratization.

Compared to many of his Arab counterparts, the king was especially successful in retaining popular support during the turbulent period of the Persian Gulf crisis and war in 1990-1991. He deftly straddled competing points of view regarding the wisdom of Saddam Hussein's invasion of Kuwait in August 1990, as well as the appropriateness of the U.S.-led response that led to the Iraqi dictator's ouster in February 1991. Hassan has demonstrated this same ingenuity in foreign affairs in his approach to Israel, which has always been pragmatic if not self-serving. Morocco was instrumental in fostering Palestinian-Israeli contacts which ultimately led to an ongoing peace process begun in earnest in 1993. Tensions have resurfaced with Algeria as that country's military coup d'état in January 1992 set back the more friendly regional relations in which Algiers had tended to indirectly acknowledge Rabat's claims to the Western Sahara. The current army-dominated regime in Algeria, uncertain of its political standing, has refocused attention on the Saharan dispute as part of its strategy of diverting public attention away from domestic grievances to so-called external threats.

The 1990s have proven to be a decade of change for Morocco. The end of the cold war, the collapse of the Soviet Union, the globalization of democracy, and the increasing interdependency of the international political economy have forced a serious rethinking about the country's strategy of political, social, and economic development. To date, the country's relatively harmonious political culture has enabled it to overcome many of the structural dislocations caused by these transforming events. Indeed, if Morocco manages to successfully conquer the inherent contradictions and conflict associated with any process of change, it will be due mainly to the adaptive political culture which has anchored Morocco's national identity over the centuries. While the monarchy may one day be fundamentally altered or disappear altogether, the nation's sense of identity will continue to endure--allowing it to make the necessary adjustments to whatever political economy challenges it may face in the future.

John P. Entelis
February 1996

Chapter One

Introduction

[The country] appears to be a happy phenomenon, unique in the third world, a prosperous liberal country. It has a parliamentary body, freely elected in the competition of a plurality of independent political parties. Its politicians are, as politicians go, relatively reasonable men. The tone of public debate is not strident. The Chamber of Deputies is an orderly assembly. Elections are conducted with a minimum of violence, and reports of coercion of the electorate are rare. [The country] enjoys freedom of association and freedom of expression. Its press is literate and not too sensational or abusive. Its citizens, freely organized, feel free to approach their parliamentary representatives either as individuals or through their organizations. It is a law-abiding country in many important respects and passions are held in check; public order is maintained without a large display of force. People do not disappear in the night, their families ignorant of where they have been taken by the police. Strikes, violent demonstrations, angry class antagonisms are relatively infrequent for a country of growing economic differentiation. Finally, the country is prosperous (Shils 1966, 1).

The good news is that the above description is a relatively accurate portrayal of contemporary Morocco. The bad news is that this is actually a Western social science assessment of pre-1975, pre–civil war Lebanon. This is not to say that Morocco is doomed to replicate Lebanon's tragedy and disintegration. It is rather to suggest that very different and competing interpretations exist as to the authenticity, profundity, and durability of Morocco's apparent success at blending political pluralism and economic development with traditional values and patrimonial cultural norms. As with Lebanon during its heyday of "ethnoconfessional democracy," Morocco arouses passionate debate

3

as to the appropriate pathway for achieving modernization and development. This book will not resolve that debate. It will, instead, provide a framework—one based on the role and relevance of "culture" as an explanatory variable—with which to understand the terms and implications of that debate. In the book, alternative scenarios will be sketched and forecasts will be offered.

Culture and politics in Morocco relate in an interactive blend of conflict and congruence producing a distinctive style of adaptive modernization in the socioeconomic sphere and incremental democratization in the political arena. With continuity and change representing Morocco's pattern of development in the more than thirty years since independence in 1956, no single cultural form adequately defines or determines the country's national identity. Instead, several cultural orientations coexist, sometimes in harmony, other times in conflict. Specifically, four distinguishable cultural patterns can be identified: monarchical, modernist, militarist, and messianic. Although these orientations both compete with and complement each other, they all share a strong and abiding affinity to an overriding cultural "core" around which revolve the three identity-forming beliefs, Islam, Arabism, and Moroccanism, creating a so-called Muslim consensus. It is this tripartite cultural core or Muslim consensus that explains much of the country's success at reconciling subcultural differences and discontinuities. Monarchical power and manipulation by themselves could not create a system of rule that is relatively pluralistic, open, and equitable by most Afro-Arab standards.

CULTURAL STRANDS

Monarchism

Monarchical culture revolves around the institution of the monarchy, which fuses both religious authority and political legitimacy. Simultaneously, the monarchy draws its legitimacy from the past by invoking Islam, Arabism, and three centuries of Alawite rule while deriving authority in the present by calling for rationalism, modern leadership, and technocracy (Geertz 1973, 248). The king's legitimacy thus derives from "intrinsic" authority—"an organic property magically ingredient in the ruler's person"—and "contractual" authority which is "conferred upon him, in some occult and complicated way, by the population he rules" (Geertz 1968, 76). "Normally" and in other places, these two traditions would be considered radically and irreconcilably opposed. But in Morocco, "where the talent for forcing things together which really do not go together is rather highly developed, they are fused if not exactly into a seamless whole at least into an integral institution which has, so far, proved quite effective in containing, even in capitalizing on, its own inner contradictions" (Geertz 1968, 76).

The full meaning of the monarchy's multiple roles in culture, society, and politics will be discussed later. It is sufficient to note here that the monarchy is the only national institution that embodies all three pillars of the Muslim consensus as part of its ongoing, active legitimization. The other cultural orientations and structures can effectively claim only portions of the cultural core. Indeed, these same structures—political parties, intellectuals, fundamentalists, the army—must attach themselves to the cultural triumvirate even as they attack, directly or indirectly, the monarchy itself or the king as an egregious violator of Morocco's national interests.

The distinctive features of the monarchical orientation are its commitment to cultural synthesis, adaptive modernization, and incremental democratization. The same contradictory traditions that have been effectively fused in creating that "peculiar" institution of the monarchy have also applied to a range of cultural dyads—secular and religious, scripturalist and saintly, Arab and Berber, urban and rural, European and African, national and parochial—which have either been synthesized or functionally harmonized. The resulting blend is a culture that is diverse at its base but uniform nationally. The fact that the relatively brief period of European colonial rule did not fundamentally disrupt the Muslim consensus but instead catalyzed and reinvigorated it in respect to the monarchy assisted the process of fusion in the postindependence period. Unlike the situation in neighboring Algeria, where the cultural "glass" was profoundly shattered as a consequence of 132 years of colonial domination, Morocco did not have to reassemble a multitude of broken pieces.

European, especially French, culture strongly influences the attitudes and behavior of the national elite without, however, impinging on its members' profound identification with and attachment to Islam, Arabism, and Moroccan nationalism. Among the elite at least, European culture has been successfully grafted onto their nationalism, creating a distinctive form of national expression that is bilingual and bicultural. For the masses, Islam, Arabism, and Moroccan nationalism remain the overwhelming bases of individual and local as well as collective identity.

In the area of socioeconomic change, monarchical culture has encouraged a reconciliatory and adaptive path for modernity consistent with the country's history and traditions. Morocco, under both King Mohamed V and King Hassan II, has maintained a synthesis between modernity and tradition as the way to modernize in a nonrevolutionary manner. Regardless of the country's level or speed of modernization, it is unlikely that modern values, norms, attitudes, and expectations will replace traditional sentiments, particularly where they are rooted and shaped in early childhood socialization. To date, and despite intermittent "outbursts" both from the masses and from above, the Moroccan system has been relatively successful in adapting universal and rational principles essential for development to the indigenous traditions necessary for national identity. As one observer has remarked, "The Western notion of development with the high premium it places on rational, secular, and universal criteria . . . are likely to remain ineffective unless they are mediated through a meaningful cultural context" (Khalaf 1968, 254). Adaptive modernization has been such a means of development via a meaningful cultural context.

Monarchical authority has been particularly sensitive to society's broad concern that, in the eagerness to be liberated from traditional constraints (felt most acutely by those living in the urban areas), there would be a simultaneous fear of losing the sense of identity afforded by time-honored and sometimes sacred traditions (Tessler 1973, 201). In brief, the policy of adaptive modernization and limited transformation has allowed Morocco to advance economically without disrupting the whole fabric of state and society (see Leveau 1979, 1985).

Incremental democratization, a gradual, step-by-step approach to political participation, equality of opportunity, and social justice, is the third component of monarchical culture. Whereas politics and governance in postindependence Morocco have experienced erratic fits of genuine yet limited democracy, alternating with extended periods of repressive authoritarianism, "the historic institutions of governance have been modernized and have been joined by modern political parties, in an institutional and cultural synthesis that is pluralistic despite its formal centralization" (Zartman 1985, 28). Although the king remains at the center of the polity, he has encouraged greater popular participation in the electoral process, especially at the local and regional levels. The subnational and parliamentary elections of 1983 and 1984, for example, are evidence that incrementalism is beginning to pay off.

Representing religious authority, state power, and charismatic personality, monarchical rule finds support among a broad segment of Moroccan society at both the elite and mass levels. Among the elite, for example, the rural bourgeoisie, the *ulama*, or religious hierarchy, elements of the urban middle class, the upper levels of the state technocracy, including key portions of the army officer class, and many in the liberal professions and private business associate themselves with the monarchical orientation and the Muslim consensus. Among the population as a whole, the vast majority of rural dwellers and peasants, along with many ordinary people in medium-sized and large cities, also identify with the Muslim consensus, which for them is embodied in the monarchy. Even segments of rural maraboutism, Sufi brotherhoods, and worshippers of saintly beings, traditionally proud of their autonomy, freedom of action, and independence from central authority, increasingly accept the throne as the legitimate symbol of national identity.

Modernism

The modernist perspective subscribes to a more visibly secular and radical formula for the development of state and society than does the monarchical culture. Two distinct components of the modernist culture exist in Morocco: liberals and leftists, or *gauchistes*. Liberals desire increased democratization, accelerated and more thorough modernization (read Westernization), and a continued commitment to biculturalism and bilingualism as expressive forms of cultural identity. The *gauchistes* demand radical democratization, state-directed and imposed modernization along explicitly socialist lines, and a more "secular" form of cultural expression. Whereas liberals could live with a brand of constitutional monarchy à la Juan Carlos of Spain, the leftists are uncompromising in their determination to eliminate the monarchy altogether. The Muslim consensus is shared by both groups, but more at the level of ideas and symbols than at the level of practice and direct application. Both tendencies of the nonmonarchical modernist culture represent a relatively small segment of Morocco's elite population: journalists, academics, intellectuals, university students, and portions of the liberal professions. Because the throne legitimizes its rule in part through appeals to its modernist goals and accomplishments, both liberals and leftists have difficulty appealing to Morocco's lower and middle classes on exclusively modernist principles. Yet the modernist culture remains an important component of the Moroccan political landscape; it alternately competes against and collaborates with the other cultural tendencies in a situation of ever-shifting alliances and political regroupments.

Militarism

The militarist orientation applies to a narrow stratum of Moroccan elite that nonetheless has the inherent capacity to impose its vision of state and society on the majority culture. The military identifies unswervingly with the Muslim consensus but fears that monarchical corruption, *gauchiste* radicalism, or Muslim fundamentalism may, alone or in combination, discredit or overthrow that consensus. Such upheaval would leave the society open to a range of abuses and uncertainties that contradict the disciplinary and law-and-order mind-set of the army officer class. Although it remains committed to modernization along

Western lines, the military is decidedly undemocratic. Its closest role model would be Francisco Franco's Spain. The militarist culture is technocratic, austere, anticorruption, disciplined, deeply conservative, and nationalistic, if not chauvinistic.

The army is convinced that it is the only "true" guardian, defined in a praetorian and paternalistic sense, of the *patrie*. In the three publicized attempts at overthrowing monarchical rule in 1971, 1972, and 1983, for example, the principal explanation for these efforts focused on the system's pervasive corruption, manipulation, and exploitation. Of relatively humble Berber-rural origin, the officer class and soldiers have come to identify themselves as the only authentic patriots in a society riddled with abuse and corruption. This Franco-style praetorianism remains an important cultural type, which neither time nor the king's special favoritism toward the army has effectively incorporated into the existing rules of the game, notwithstanding the numerous advantages that the king has gained from his policy in the Western Sahara. Although the king's pursuit of Saharan annexation has the full support of the army, whose power and prestige has been enhanced as a consequence of its impressive battlefield successes, this support does not mean that the army might not turn against him in the future. In brief, the militarist perspective is antidemocratic, modernist in a technical rather than a social-cultural sense, and supportive of the Muslim consensus understood in a paternalistic and exclusivist rather than collaborationist way.

Messianism

The messianic perspective is the fourth and potentially most "disruptive" of Morocco's competing cultures. Messianism, conceived as a belief in the absolute rightness of a cause, is not new either to Morocco or to the Arab-Islamic world as a whole. What is new, however, is the way in which the faith is being interpreted, the types of organizations that have been created to apply it, the new clientele and supporters that Islamic fundamentalism has attracted, and the distinctive way in which fundamentalists, *intégristes*, have forged a synthesis with modern political ideas and instrumentalities (see Etienne 1987).

The messianic thrust is antimodern and "democratic" in an authoritarian rather than pluralistic sense, recalling Talmon's concept of "totalitarian democracy" (1965). The neo-Muslim orientation reluctantly accepts the Muslim consensus in its present form; its preference would be that Islam be disaggregated from the Arab and Moroccan components. In this sense Islam is defined in a totalistic way applicable to all believers, regardless of language or nationality, who accept the need to live out and act upon an exclusively Muslim ideal. Although nowhere in Morocco is militant Islam so influential or powerful a force as it is in nearby Algeria and Tunisia, for example, it is beginning to attract a diverse category of people who possess skills, influence, and capacities to have a significant impact on state and society sometime in the future.

Unlike "traditional" Islamic movements, which were organized on the basis of traditional schools of law or Sufi brotherhoods, the fundamentalists are based on study groups, scout movements, women's auxiliaries, athletic clubs, economic enterprises, political parties, and paramilitary units (Lapidus 1983, 44). These radical movements also appeal to a new clientele: "in part to the bazaar, or old middle-class elements, displaced by economic and political change, and in part to the modern educated intelligentsia" (Lapidus 1983, 44).

Most significantly, and very much unlike "traditional" Islam which played only a limited part in politics, revivalist Islam takes "the deep psychological needs for faith and fellowship and projects them into political causes. Religious belief, solidarity, and feelings are more and more channeled into politics, and political actions are more and more based on religious concepts and loyalties" (Lapidus 1983, 46). The merging of religion and politics has always been viewed as an Islamic ideal. Only in the recent era, however, are they actually being fused together.

Another important characteristic of messianic movements in Morocco is that they express both personal religious and collective political goals with the same condensed symbols. They directly link personal morality to political action. The condensation of individual and political expectations in the same symbolic language allows the *intégristes* to operate across a broad spectrum of concerns. "They preach individual morality; they espouse educational improvements and social welfare; and they aspire to control state economic policies and foreign affairs to realize Islamic goals" (Lapidus 1983, 48).

Because monarchical power is so deeply rooted in religious legitimacy, the throne has been able to neutralize much of the appeal of Islamic-oriented messianic movements. As a consequence, the latter remain publicly committed to the Muslim consensus however much they may disagree with the throne on the issues of socioeconomic modernization and political development.

THE MUSLIM CONSENSUS

These four cultural orientations coexist under conditions of cooperation and conflict, with the monarchical culture dominating Moroccan political life. The throne's intimate identification with the Muslim consensus has enabled it to pursue successfully policies of cultural synthesis, adaptive modernization, and incremental democratization, which remain the hallmarks of Moroccan politics and power in the twentieth century. In their attempts to modify or overtake monarchical power, the competing cultures must provide an alternate paradigm that is consistent with existing cultural values, yet capable of providing material improvements in a nondisruptive manner. As one analyst has commented: "Any society contains competing discourses, which are not internally consistent and which are filled with tensions and ambiguities. In Morocco, these competing voices are unequally weighted. Activists in organized political groups and Islamic militants each seek a departure from the accepted status quo. As such they must consciously articulate and win acceptance for wide-ranging reorientations towards politics and society" (Eickelman 1985, 179).

In summary, the Muslim consensus defines and distinguishes Morocco's cultural identity. This consensus is based on three interrelated concepts: (1) Islam animates the nation's spiritual life and anchors its social existence. It is nearly universal, "and no aspect of life fails to feel the influence of this powerful religion, which is ever present in the thoughts and activities of the population" (Nelson 1978, 103). (2) Arabism fuses language, culture, history, and nationality into an integrated whole; it is shared by virtually all Moroccans whether Arabic- or Berber-speaking in origin. (3) Moroccanism or Moroccan nationalism is that specific nationalist sentiment that focuses citizen loyalty on Morocco as state, nation, territory, and ideal; one state, having its own distinctive identity and historic independence.

The deep territorial and tribal divisions that once separated the *bled al-makhzan* (lands under government control) from the *bled as-siba* (dissident, tribal lands) have been effectively overcome in the modern period, creating among contemporary Moroccans a strong sense of nationalist identity. The facts that Ottoman suzerainty never reached Morocco and that European colonial rule was relatively brief add to this proud sense of authentic independence and historic longevity. The incorporation of the Western Sahara into Morocco proper since 1975, for example, can be understood only in the context of this proud nationalist tradition with which virtually all Moroccans identify. For many Moroccans the monarchy itself constitutes a fourth legitimate pillar of the Muslim consensus.

These components are subsumed under the label "Muslim" consensus because, for the overwhelming majority of Moroccans, "religious authority both transcends and suffuses national identity" (Munson 1984, 49). The fact that Moroccans refer to themselves as "Muslims," however, does not mean that their sense of national identity is weak (Laroui 1980, 59). Indeed, the opposite is the case, for, unlike the situation in the West where religious and national identities have been kept legally separate, in Morocco, as in other parts of the Arab-Islamic world, legally and culturally Islam and nationalism are simply two forms of a collective identity, thus creating the term *Muslim consensus*.

Whereas the Muslim consensus defines Morocco's cultural core, four subcultural orientations compete in an attempt to give practical meaning to that consensus in the cultural, social, economic, and political spheres. (In the countryside and at the local level, maraboutism, or saintly worship, is considered by some to be an additional cultural orientation). Indeed, the distinguishing characteristic of each orientation centers on the way society and polity evolve, consistent with the tripartite ideals of the Muslim consensus. Since independence, the monarchical orientation has dominated state and society in Morocco. Working from a base of charismatic, traditional, and religious legitimacy, King Hassan has pursued policies of synthesis, fusion, adaptiveness, and incrementalism that, along with the many positive and negative sanctions available to him in the form of patronage and coercive capabilities, have ensured a relatively unchallenged political supremacy for nearly three decades. Yet challenges have never been fully eliminated, and they continue to appear in the present, as they will most likely continue in the future. Ultimately the fate of culture and politics in Morocco will rest on how the monarchy handles challenges to the system from within and without. Why have these challenges emerged? Under what conditions? With what consequences?

SYSTEM CHALLENGES

Since independence, Morocco has experienced intermittent challenges to its rule via different, often unrelated, forms of popular discontent as expressed in demonstrations, attempted coups, riots, strikes, and uprisings. Rural rebellions were suppressed in 1958 and 1972, a brief and inconclusive border war with Algeria occurred in 1963, several plots and unsuccessful military coups—both alleged and real—took place in 1963, 1971, 1972, 1973, and 1983, and urban riots and mass demonstrations involving much violence and death swept the country in 1965, 1977, 1981, and 1984. There have been many other forms of sociopolitical protest among students, laborers, and the urban unemployed, along with unconfirmed attempts at state takeover by the military. By most Third World standards, neither the frequency nor the scope or intensity of these "outbursts" has been particularly excessive. Yet they remain challenges nonetheless that, in some instances, have been very close to overthrowing royal authority and, with it, the cultural foundation upon which monarchical rule has been established.

For over thirty years Morocco has represented a classic case of socioeconomic change far outdistancing political development.

Whereas the gap between the two remained relatively manageable in the 1950s and 1960s, it began to widen sharply in the 1970s and 1980s, leading some to believe that the system was ripe for revolution.

The monarch and the monarchy are at the center of politics in Morocco despite the existence of certain pluralistic features, including a multiparty system, autonomous interest groups, independent unions, a free press. The king relies on his traditional legitimacy—as commander of the faithful, *sharif* (descendant of the Prophet), member of the Alawite dynasty, possessor of *baraka*, or personal charisma, and symbol of the nationalist struggle—to retain the support of the masses. In addition, however, monarchical supremacy has depended upon existing social pluralism and divisions among the country's elite.

The king's power and prestige are further enhanced by the fact that he is the nation's most prominent dispenser of patronage and the ultimate source of spoils in the system. The palace has a very real command over Moroccan commercial activities as well as over the distribution of patronage, both of which it uses to sustain the king's secular clientele and to build his secular alliances. Indeed, these commercial and patronage resources are the king's most effective levers of political control.

Inasmuch as Moroccan society consists of numerous segments that have historically related to one another by tension and conflict, one of the most important political roles in the country has been that of the king as arbiter among conflicting groups. This role has also helped to make the monarch the pivotal center of Morocco's disparate and factionalized political arena. In this system of patrimonialism, the king uses his virtual monopoly over major political appointments to play off one group against another, now rewarding this faction, now the other. It is a subtle power game in which the dominant aim is to prevent the crystallization of serious opposition to the palace.

If all else fails, power and control can be maintained by the king's loyal lieutenants. An executive staff, the intelligence and security branches of the Ministry of the Interior and the Ministry of National Defense, as well as the army and officer corps all assist in the maintenance of royal authority throughout the kingdom.

The past and current success of royal control has therefore centered on the ability of the king to manipulate the elite while maintaining broad support from the rural masses, who still constitute nearly 60 percent of Morocco's total population of close to twenty-five million. In combination, this has permitted the king to pursue his goals of cultural synthesis, adaptive modernization, and incremental democratization.

As long as the elite remains small—in 1982 it was estimated to be around one thousand (Tessler 1982)—socially and educationally homogeneous, and politically fragmented, the system has fairly good prospects for maintaining power. However, the size of the elite and the balance of its component parts cannot be guaranteed in the future. On the contrary, rapid population and educational growth will inevitably threaten the equilibrium at all social levels, including that of the elite. The implications of this long-term demographic process for the monarchy's hegemonic role are clear. Over time, Morocco will have to broaden the base of participation in the political process if it is to maintain political stability and development. Yet, if it does so, there is the danger that an expanded political class will overwhelm the resources of the patronage system controlled by the palace, thereby exceeding its absorptive capacity and destabilizing the political system from within.

The present system can also be expected to come under pressure from nonelite sectors of society. Economic and political grievances, which are growing among the masses, may ultimately erode the legitimacy accorded to the monarchy and become the most salient dimension of public attitudes toward authority. Such pressures have already made themselves felt, in the rioting of 1981 and 1984, for example. Though limited to the urban poor, these disturbances are a strong indication that the masses are beginning to demand greater accountability from the king and his government, and that they may no longer respond to symbolic appeals based on historic or religious criteria.

The adaptive and incremental components of monarchical rule will be coming under increased pressure as the full implications of vast demographic and socioeconomic changes begin to be felt. In the three decades since independence the Moroccan social landscape has changed dramatically: The population has doubled, with 70 percent under thirty and 42 percent under fifteen years of age. The urban population is expanding rapidly; it is expected to reach 50 percent by the end of the 1990s. Additionally, large numbers inhabit the sprawling bidonvilles that attach themselves to the periphery of Morocco's largest cities, especially Casablanca. Education is booming, with nearly four million students at all levels of the educational system and a third of government expenditures being devoted to schooling and health. Scores of schools are being built annually, yet never quickly enough to keep up with demand. Literacy rates are increasing (40 percent in 1987), with all the implications this has on incipient political consciousness and desire for extended participation. Economically the country is still considered "poor" in statistical terms at least. It is estimated, for example, that 2.5 million out of the country's 3.1 million households live on less than $110 a month, which is considered below the "absolute poverty" line established by the World Bank (see Eickelman 1986, 187). Official unemployment ranges from 20 percent to 30 percent in the cities and probably averages 40 percent or more in the rural areas. Underemployment also remains a serious problem.

One must be careful, however, not to exaggerate the social significance of demographic statistics or to correlate too directly their implications on the potential for political violence. The necessary ingredients needed for an "explosion" to take place in Morocco, for example, are so widespread throughout the Afro-Arab world—overpopulation, overurbanization, unemployment, derelict social services, inadequate schooling, social inequality,—that they offer little in the way of predictive power. Additionally, Morocco's "on the ground" reality of daily existence belies the bleak statistical profile of the country. The fact of the matter is that for most Moroccans living in the cities and in the countryside the quality of life is infinitely superior to what it was two decades ago. For many in the urban middle class especially, daily life is beginning to approximate that of Greece, Spain, and Portugal of the 1950s in terms of consumer goods available and access to urban amenities. Unlike daily life in other parts of the Maghreb, denizens of Morocco's cities enjoy many fruits of developed society, including relatively clean and efficient transportation systems, movies, bookstores, libraries, restaurants, parks, hospitals, and other elements of "civilized" urban existence that make cities attractive places in which to live and work. Even the bidonvilles are slowly being razed, to be replaced by tasteful and modestly comfortable working-class housing. This contrasts sharply with the East European–like "block factories" that one finds in Algeria's northern cities (see Leveau 1985; Entelis 1986).

These things notwithstanding, however, centralized political authority, economic uncertainty, and a narrow base for genuine political participation all constitute serious challenges to monarchical rule and a real threat to "the whole mixture of the West and Islam that [the king's] regime represents" (Zartman 1985, 30).

There is preliminary evidence nonetheless that the monarchy is beginning to respond to these simultaneous challenges in creative and effective ways. Economic improvements have been aided by the end of a devastating drought and the continued low price of imported oil. The political process is opening up, especially at the local and regional levels, where the government has devoted needed financial and support services to make this process a reality (Nellis 1983). Policies of Arabizing education and administration are gaining the support of monolingual Arabists in the countryside and in the cities. The monarchy continues to take its Islamic identity very seriously in both deeds and symbols, thus reducing the appeal of more radical Muslim movements that continue to attack the throne's policy of cultural synthesis. Finally, in regional and international affairs, the monarchy has maintained the advantage over all other groups, especially with its successful campaign of incorporating the Western Sahara into Morocco proper.

The central question this book seeks to answer is whether these positive efforts are simply the result of a combination of good fortune, monarchical ingenuity, and inept opposition or whether they are genuinely congruent with Morocco's core culture as interpreted and applied by the monarchy. If it is the former, then one can expect the existing competing subcultures to transform themselves quickly into countercultures. As such, each would seek to co-opt for itself exclusively the Muslim consensus and provide its own interpretation of how that consensus should be "correctly" applied. The progressive, praetorian, and puritanical cultural alternatives will each be evaluated in turn as possible substitutes to the mainstream and dominant culture now in power.

THEORETICAL ALTERNATIVES:
POLITICAL CULTURE VERSUS
POLITICAL ECONOMY

As referred to in the beginning of this chapter, interpreters of Morocco's development tend to divide rather distinctly, although unevenly, between those who look exclusively to the country's internal processes for explanation as to the pattern of national development being pursued (see Ashford 1961a; Combs-Schilling 1982; Damis 1972 1975; Eickelman 1976, 1985, 1986; Leveau 1985; Tessler 1982; Zartman 1964) and those who place virtually the whole explanatory weight for the country's "underdevelopment" upon external factors such as imperialism and other forms of capitalist world domination (see Amin 1970; Hodges 1983; Paul 1975; Seddon 1984).

According to this latter perspective, indigenous leaders are nothing but "liaison-elite providing linkages between the center and the periphery of the capitalist economy. The liaison-elite and their class basis are presumed to have internalized a legacy of dependency because they have a vested interest in its sustenance" (Hermassi 1972, 217). Such a view denies the national elite any meaningful scope for independent or autonomous action. Indeed, each step in the implementation of Third World development strategies and in the relationships of such politics with outside powers is "preprogrammed by the 'world capitalist system'" (Waterbury 1983, 4).

There is no compelling evidence to accept on face value this proposition, which, in many of its arguments, is nothing more than ideology disguised as science. Increasingly, Marxian, *dependencia*, and world capitalist theories about the Third World "have become bogged down in a seemingly endless multiplication of exercises in mode-of-productionism and world-systematics in which the distinctive features of each country simply disappear and all become look-alikes, only distinguished from one another insofar as some are central, others peripheral or semi-peripheral" (Worsley 1984, 41).

As more empirical evidence becomes available to analysts of Third World development, it is increasingly clear that neither approach by itself is sufficient to explain developmental patterns. Even one well-known scholar's transformation from "political culturalist" (Waterbury 1970) to "political economist" (Waterbury 1983) has not led to an exclusivist interpretation of political behavior. Instead, John Waterbury, in his study of Egypt under Gamal Abdel Nasser and Anwar Sadat, for example, acknowledged the need to look at internal processes, such as culture and domestic economic variables, as well as those factors of dependency that force many countries to turn to external sources of finance capital, technology, markets, and arms as a means for achieving internal development (1983, 4). Similarly, a North African sociologist has noted that, in order to understand variations in national development, analysts "must study historical backwardness and the specific consequences of world domination" (Hermassi 1972, 216).

The difficulty with such approaches and recommendations, however, is that although they are conceptually persuasive, the many variables that would have to be identified, correlated, and analyzed would be extremely difficult to put into operation. More appropriately, as in the case of Morocco, one can refer to a political economy "input"—that is, the direct and indirect impact and influence of the "world class system" on state and society—and a political culture "output"—namely, a response to such inputs based on indigenous features of culture, history, and national values. In other words, the external-internal variables could be dichotomized into input-related factors in which the external environment, especially its powerful economic component, would be viewed as having a direct if not determinative impact on the capital value of resources extant in a country and the manner in which it can profit from them; the output dimension would apply to the kinds of policy choices available to a regime in which general culture, political culture, and the domestic socioeconomic makeup of the country would be most relevant.

Despite the global impact of capitalism and industrialization, countries like Morocco utilize their own frameworks and responses. The policies of the World Bank and the International Monetary Fund (IMF), for example, do not create uniform outputs; the latter are much more influenced by cultural rather than economic or "rational" factors. As one Middle East historian has accurately observed: "Islamic societies shall continue to feel the impact of forces originating in the West, such as capitalism and industrialization, and so on. However, the cultural and social organizational responses of Muslim Middle Eastern society to the structural changes generated by contact with the West are derived from its own culture and from its own ways of reacting to outside challenge" (Karpat 1986, 12).

This study will identify the critical features of the external environment and incorporate them into an analysis that is principally directed at the kinds of policy alternatives available to Morocco in its quest to modernize and develop and for which culture and culturally related historic and domestic socioeconomic factors are most directly relevant.

The remaining portions of this study will be organized along the following lines: General cultural patterns relating to individual as well as collective orientations will be identified in Chapter 2, with a particular focus on values associated with Islam in its varied manifestations. Chapter 3 will relate culture to politics according to a threefold categorization: cognitive, evaluative, and affective. Mass and elite attitudes toward political life as well as the way Moroccan politics operates and affects people will be discussed. The role of the monarchy in this regard is particularly important, as is the "pragmatic" character of political action. More than in other parts of the Arab world, symbolic politics plays an important role in legitimizing political life and thus will receive special attention.

The country's various subcultures will be introduced in Chapter 4 and broken down according to masses, elites, and institutions. An assessment of the competing subcultures—modernist, militarist, messianic, and less so, maraboutic—will be made. The chapter will also explore the relationship of culture to foreign policy decisionmaking and present evidence to show the relatively weak linkage between the two.

Chapter 5 will deal with political socialization processes, including the role of institutions and the impact of international influences. Surprisingly, there are a number of survey studies on Morocco that provide partial empirical substantiation for the socialization patterns described. Chapter 6 will identify the sources and configurations of countercultural trends that may evolve to challenge the dominant culture. Finally, this study will conclude with a summary of its findings, from which specific alternative regimes will be identified and assessed.

Chapter Two

General
Cultural Patterns

Moroccan society is diverse but not divided. It is a country of "profound cultural diversity and separate human landscapes in which the legacy of distinctive cultural development remains strong" (Miller 1984, 28). Yet it is also a society securely integrated within the framework of a modernizing state. Moroccan life is governed by an intricate and complex interaction of social and physical features in which the traditional and modern are intertwined into a mosaic or, more appropriately, an arabesque.

The historically determined, traditionally rooted, and colonially encouraged axes crosscutting Moroccan society are no longer so salient as they once were in describing cultural patterns in the country. To be sure, male-female, urban-rural, sedentary-nomadic, secular-religious, scripturalist-saintly, and Arab-Berber differences remain as socioanthropological categories relevant to daily existence. But, increasingly, rather than being viewed as conflictual dyads, these axes are best understood as complementary parts of a single cultural tradition. Despite French attempts to exploit these apparent differences through a policy of divide and rule, culture and society remain intact. Differences based on distinctive tribal or ethnic identities play themselves out at the personal and local levels, with limited implications for the integrity of the national state.

The latter situation is probably best represented by Morocco's diverse Berber tribes, which constitute an estimated 40 percent of the total Moroccan population. The fact that the Berbers are the original inhabitants of North Africa, preceding Arabs and Islam, is not mirrored in the folk mind. Moroccan Berbers, like their counterparts in Algeria, see themselves as members of this or that tribe, "within an Islamically conceived and permeated world—and *not* as members of a linguistically defined ethnic group, in a world in which Islam is but one thing among others" (Gellner 1972b, 13).

The tribe constitutes the "social organizer of local land and life, [a] powerful repository of past experience, and [a] vehicle through which people meet the challenges of every day life in concert"; but it is Islam that is the "source of spiritual coherence, philosophy, and explanation of individual destinies and contemporary opportunities" (Miller 1984, 6). In other words, subcultural cleavages are superseded by the triple bastions of civilization and identity in Morocco—Islam, Arabism, and Moroccanism—which form a Muslim consensus. These pillars of culture were the ideological focuses of anticolonial nationalism before independence and are central to the identity of Moroccan society today. It is in the context of this Muslim consensus that the following discussion of personal and collective cultural patterns will be presented.

THE MOROCCAN PERSONALITY

Any attempt to describe "personality traits" of a society as varied and culturally rich as Morocco is fraught with obvious dangers and pitfalls. There is no such thing as a typical Moroccan and therefore no typical pattern of personality-based culture. The best one can expect is to identify extremely broad orientations from which can be made linkages with culture in general and political culture in particular. Probably the most significant differences in orientations can be found between urban and rural dwellers, men and women, and the educated and the illiterate. Inasmuch as we are looking for common cultural traits across the full landscape of Moroccan society, these dichotomous social groupings will be introduced only where significant differences in orientation exist.

In assessing the literature on "Arab personality" traits and values, several researchers have assembled a compendium of essentially negative and deficient characteristics: suspiciousness, excessive hostility alternating with excessive politeness, negative individualism, a large reservoir of free-floating hostility, efforts to keep conflicts suppressed or at least manageable, a high degree of mistrust and hostility toward others, secretiveness about the self and curiosity about others, and, as a result of the unpredictable and arbitrary patterns of parental relations with children, a resulting wish to ingratiate oneself with those in authority (see Ben Dor 1977; Berger 1964; Patai 1976; Ammar 1966; Moughrabi 1978).

A noted sociologist of Arab society, in describing the traits of interpersonal relations among Arabs, produced his own list: encouragement of sibling rivalry, lack of trust and weakness of cooperation outside of the family and other primordial units, formality and rigidity, political quietism (acceptance of fate in life in general and in politics in particular), authoritarianism, a disinclination to look into the unknown, and an unwillingness to acknowledge the enormous gap between the ideal and the real (see Berger 1964, chapter 5). In sum, the personality pattern that emerges from this and other research focuses on charac-teristics such as free-floating hostility, rigidity, the lack of reality testing, and suspiciousness (Moughrabi 1978, 99).

The context in which most of this sociopsychological research takes place is the quest for explanation as to why Arab society is not "rational," "modern," or "democratic." The collective traits associated with modernity—"individuality, creativity, the em-pirical attitude, the criterion of efficiency, an indifference to or disbelief in the efficacy of supernational forces, the freedom of the individual, economic progress, a concern for national unity and dignity, and an interest in the larger world" (Shils 1968, 31–32)—are supposedly lacking or minimally present in the Arab world. For sociopsychologists the principle explanation for this condition is found in Arab child-rearing practices, social-ization processes, and behavioral norms.

Given the importance of religion and family in such tra-ditional societies, some scholars have focused on these structures as the source of the "problem." Reviewing the interpretation of one Western-trained Arab social scientist, Moughrabi summa-rized the former's arguments as follows:

Religion tends to maintain . . . absolutist values which influence social relations in such a way as to make it difficult for the individual to distinguish between goals and means, to be tolerant, critical, innovative. Another by-product of absolutist values is fatalism which generates passivity, capitulation, and lack of ambition. The family is too binding in its social demands and too restricting of the individual. It exacts from him absolute loyalty, thereby sacrificing autonomy and self-reliance in favor of obedience and the reliance on others. In the Arab world there is little emphasis on psychological rewards and punishments that tend to favor the growth of conscience. Rather, there is frequent use of corporal punishment, of shaming techniques, and fear of unknown spiritual monsters. Finally, Arab society is more spontaneous than calculating and more socioemotionally oriented than it is task-oriented. A society that cannot delay gratification, the Arab world is also more preoccupied with status than with achievement (1978, 109).

Without getting bogged down in the many theoretical and normative assumptions associated with such controversial studies, one can agree that some of the traits described above do apply to large categories of Arab, as well as non-Arab, people. What remains in doubt, however, is whether or not such sociopsychologically determined patterns are actual stumbling blocks on the path to modernization and development or merely obstacles to the achievement of a certain kind of modernization and development? The case of Morocco in this regard may be instructive.

PRIMORDIALISM

A leading interpreter of Moroccan development has focused his attention on primordial beliefs and practices found in traditional tribal society, using them as a basis for understanding and explaining interpersonal and intergroup relations as they manifest themselves in the society as a whole and in the political arena in particular. According to this perspective, although the heavily secular, bicultural, and bilingual national elite, for example, is not "tribal," its behavior is very much dictated by the values of segmentary tribal society that the elite has internalized. The following traditional Moroccan values are said to have direct applicability to culture in general and political culture specifically:

> (1) segmentary patterns of social relationships, whereby individuals view themselves as members of intersecting corporate entities (linked in traditional society by alleged patrilineal descent) that divide and coalesce depending on the degree of external challenge; (2) a related view that the manipulation of kinshiplike sentiments for sociopolitical objectives is appropriate and legitimate; (3) and a belief that the purpose of alliance-building and manipulation is to minimize dependence on others while maximizing personal autonomy and authority (Tessler 1982, 65).

For John Waterbury, writing in 1970, these values, which originate in the tribal context, have direct relevance to those in the modern sector. As a result, the behavior of elite and nonelite, modern and traditional, secular and religious, are all founded upon a shared cultural tradition (1970). In other words, Morocco's social and cultural heritage has direct influence on the dominant role of patron-client relationships and segmented alliances as they manifest themselves in national political life (Tessler 1982, 65).

Morocco's shared cultural tradition manifests both functional and dysfunctional characteristics, as they relate to the processes of social and political development. The cultural orientation of the secular elite, for example, continues to be characterized by a common commitment to traditional norms as they apply to community, family, religion, and male-female relations. Though trained in modern professions such as medicine, law, engineering, and military science, the country's educated elite adheres to a "new traditionalism" that ties them to the cultural norms and values of the broader society (Waterbury 1970, 8).

The defense-minded character of Moroccan behavior, which is also rooted in traditional tribal values, has more negative consequences. In the modern setting it is reflected in the practice of constant building of alliances, which begins with one's own family. Alliances are forever being formed and then cemented through financial and moral debts. Moroccans devote an excessive amount of time and energy to buttressing this alliance system; every individual assumes it is the preoccupation of all others. The actors demonstrate remarkable restraint in the way they exercise power and press victories. Decisive gains are never achieved and a balance between alliances is maintained; one never knows when today's enemy may be tomorrow's ally (Moore 1971).

The origin of this mind-set is found in tribal behavior. Historically, tribal solidarity in Morocco resulted less from common ancestral ties, loyalty to a single leader, or a sense of collective purpose, although each or all of these attributes were often invoked, than from the complex of tension, friction, and hostility extant among the tribe's component parts. Paradoxically, while such tensions created hostility, feuds, and even moments of intertribal warfare, the overall effect was to maintain and advance, not destroy, the tribal structure (Waterbury 1970, 62).

This paradox is clarified through an explanation of segmentary tribal structures in which internal equilibrium is seldom achieved or long maintained. However, neither are severe power imbalances within given units in the system long tolerated (Waterbury 1970, 65).

In the contemporary situation Waterbury identified three types of segmental factions in Morocco: those founded on primordial attachments, those factions displaying a blend of objective interests and primordial attachments (mixed or clientelist factions), and those defined exclusively according to objective interests (interest-oriented factions) (1970, 69).

Primordial factions include tribes, religion, regions (sometimes), cities and city neighborhoods, and families. Collectively, they constitute overlapping pieces of a "vast segmentary mosaic" that made up and continue to characterize traditional Morocco (Waterbury 1970, 69). Regardless of segmentary factions, all Moroccan behavior, political or otherwise, is framed in terms of the defensive use of power and authority. In this context it is not unusual to see a Moroccan use power to protect and preserve what he already has rather than as a means to "act positively, create, destroy, or strike out in new directions" (Waterbury 1970, 74–75).

The presence of a defensive orientation and the concurrent need to establish and maintain alliances are rooted in a group mentality that itself flows from segmentary tribal structures. Throughout history the group orientation predominated in Morocco, and individuals as such could have little influence in society. Originating from this historical context, Moroccans today conceive of themselves or others "acting autonomously with difficulty, and they feel comfortable only when integrated into a group. . . . A man must have a group, for otherwise he is without defenses, and no man is willingly defenseless. It is in relation to the group that the Moroccan defines himself, and without the group he loses his identity" (Waterbury 1970, 76–77).

In a defense-oriented world, alliance building and alliance maintenance are crucial to survival. The goal is never to be outmaneuvered or duped into a defenseless position. In politics, as in other dimensions of social existence, "covert machinations, dissimulation, and trickery are accepted as the facts of . . . life, and a man's ostensible motives for a given action cannot be trusted. In his dealings with others . . . the Moroccan takes for granted an element of conspiracy" (Waterbury 1970, 77). This latter characteristic is applicable to virtually all levels of social and political interaction—local, national, international.

That Moroccan society has not collapsed under the weight of these tensions and conflicts is explained by the balance-of-power system inherent in the segmentation process itself. Indeed these divisive forces have long served as catalysts to group cohesion rather than group disintegration. "Segmentation combined with shared interests—the interplay of animosity and dependency among units—[is evident throughout Moroccan society]" (Waterbury 1970, 161).

Contradictions in personality behavior and social norms create individuals who are basically suspicious, distrustful, cynical, and wary of the new, unknown, or untested. Collectively such traits are deemed as harmful to functional development as they are inimical to cooperativist efforts so necessary to overcome the problems of "backwardness," whether social, economic, or political.

Similar observations have been made by other scholars analyzing somewhat different societies, such as Algeria and Iran, that share a common Muslim–Middle East background and identity. Algerians, for example, have been described as manifesting "considerable hostility and mistrust" (Quandt 1969, 266). Not only does Algerian political culture reveal a high degree of conflict among individuals and groups "but also . . . the personality of each Algerian is marked by deep contradictions" (Quandt 1969, 265). Like their Moroccan counterparts, Algerians display distrust, suspicion, and *méfiance* toward others in and out of positions of power and authority (see Entelis 1981). Rather than originating in the context of tribal segmentary patterns, Algerian distrust and cynicism are the result of discontinuous socialization processes experienced by different segments of elite and nonelite during the lengthy and profoundly disruptive precolonial, colonial, and postcolonial phases of Algerian social history (Entelis 1986).

Further east, Marvin Zonis has recorded a similar pattern of cynicism, mistrust, manifest insecurity, and interpersonal exploitation on the part of Iranian elites who themselves mirror broader shared cultural orientations (1971). In Iran, as in Morocco, training in dissimulation begins early in life and continues throughout the overall socialization process. It is such training in hiding or masking one's own personal thought that contributes to the marked instability in interpersonal relations and is also at the "root of the distrust so prevalent throughout the society" (Zonis 1971, 270). Mistrust in interpersonal relations is a key factor in limiting cooperation essential for organization and development, whether at the local or national level. Cynicism and mistrust are characteristic ethics of Moroccan, Algerian, and Iranian societies, applicable to all interpersonal relations, including those involving immediate and direct family members.

What is one to make of these complementary sociopsychological interpretations of behavioral norms in which common inputs have resulted in dramatically different outputs? In the examples studied, the problem seems not to be with the theoretical or empirical validity of the variables themselves but with the way in which they have been interpreted and applied. In other words, that (prerevolutionary) Iran more dramatically and Algeria less visibly have had difficulties in transforming state and society along modernist lines has much to do with the inappropriateness of the models of development being utilized. There is nothing inherently dysfunctional in a society in which cynicism and distrust exist as personality norms if such factors are incidental to the process of social change taking place. But if a "rationalistic," secular, Western-inspired model of modernization and development is introduced in which such characteristics are directly or indirectly antithetical to that model, then it is clear that difficulties will arise. In both Iran and Algeria secular political leaders were unwilling either to transform the general culture to fit the modernist framework or to modify the model significantly so as to make it more congruent with the existing culture. The results have been obvious—social revolution in one, social stalemate in the other.

Morocco, in contrast, has attempted to modify both culture and political economy through incremental policies while utilizing the powerful legitimizing intermediary of Islam—the Muslim consensus—as a means to buffer man, state, and society from the natural traumas of social change. This interpretation is being given further validation by the developments taking place in Tunisia. For over thirty years Tunisia's highly Westernized elite has sought to apply, through exhortation, propaganda, and intimidation, a model of modernization and development directly at odds with the traditional societal base, of which Islamic identity is at the center. Since political culture was never fundamentally transformed and the religious idiom was not given a truly legitimizing role, vast cleavages between elites and masses have developed (see Entelis 1974). As a recent study has shown, it is neither the desire for significant economic development nor the demand for greater participation in the political process that explains why more and more Tunisians are turning toward Islam (Waltz 1986). Rather it is a sociopsychological response to the elite-imposed "foreign" culture borrowed from the West that has created a deep sense of personal alienation and collective disenchantment. The "constitutional" overthrow of the three-decade-old Habib Bourguiba regime in late 1987 has not significantly altered this cultural crisis, whatever else it may have done for political opportunity in the state.

To summarize, unlike the situations in prerevolutionary Iran and contemporary Algeria and Tunisia, Morocco is following a reconciliatory path in which traditional identities and cultural norms are being fused with the instrumental needs of economic and political development through a tripartite policy of cultural synthesis, adaptive modernization, and incremental democratization. The central legitimizing instrument is the Muslim consensus, which the monarchy has so far succeeded in incorporating as part of its own legitimacy. By themselves, aggregates of dysfunctional personality traits, behavioral norms, and cultural orientations do not explain system stalemate or breakdown. Indeed, to the extent that these same traits are rooted in traditional practices—tribal segmentation, for example—the more functional social change will be. In any case, such factors tend to "wash out" where more compelling cultural identities exist, as with Islam. It is to this broader cultural configuration that we now turn.

ISLAM

Islam provides a strong bond that brings together Moroccans, regardless of ethnolinguistic, regional, or tribal differences in a fellowship constructed upon faith in one God. As already indicated, Islamic belief animates the spiritual life of Morocco and provides the foundation for the country's traditional social system. Since its introduction into the Maghreb in the seventh century A.D., Islam has evolved and interacted with the indigenous predominantly Berber culture to produce a style of religious belief and practice that is uniquely Moroccan. Both Arabs and Berbers are profoundly Islamicized, and it is this deep Islamic consciousness that exercises a virtual veto power over the whole realm of political action in the state (see Moore 1970).

Although Islam orients public and private life in both modern and traditional milieus, it is in the countryside, in the hundreds of small towns and villages that dot the rural landscapes of

Morocco, that the faith is expressed with particular fervor and its impact is all-encompassing. One observer of rural Morocco has provided the following sensitive portrayal of the personal base of Islam.

> [Islam] marks days, months, years and the passages of lifetimes. It envelops human conversation through ritualized salutations that mark the beginning and ending of interpersonal communications. It comes in calls from the mosque, the sounds of the rifle that end the day's fasting during Ramadan, in the spilling of blood on the Aid (the festive holiday marking the end of the fast of Ramadan), in the bustle of food, people and light on the Night of Revelation. Islam is part of the framework within which people organize, live, lament, celebrate and contemplate their lives (Combs-Schilling 1982, 14).

Manifest acts of common worship strengthen the awareness of one Muslim for the other in times of prosperity or adversity. In many respects such acts serve to cement communal bonds by stimulating the individual's sense of belonging. Meeting the devotional requirements of the faith is the basic prerequisite of becoming a Muslim.

The basic symbols of Islam in ritual and everyday life, forming the five principles of the faith, are

- *shahadah:* the attestation of faith ("There is no god but God")
- *salah:* ritual prayer, undertaken five times a day
- *zakat:* almsgiving
- *sawm:* fasting during Ramadan
- *hajj:* the pilgrimage to Mecca that every believer, if physically and financially able, is required to undertake at least once in a lifetime

Traditionalists obey as many of these five ceremonial duties as possible, modernists as few—yet both remain "devout" Muslims.

This devoutness is no paradox but consistent with the commonsense perspective that Islam exhibits. Eickelman has defined five key Islamic concepts through which traditional

Moroccans comprehend social experience and give meaning to daily existence. These five concepts are God's will ("focuses man's attention on the empirical social order by attenuating speculation on other possible orders"), reason ("enables man to perceive this order and discern what is in their best interest"), propriety ("possession of self-control which enables men to act properly in the social order"), obligation ("the nature of obligations contracted by men determines and maintains their social honor in relation to other men"), and compulsion ("a means of restoring serious breaks in the web of obligations which bind men together") (1976, 124; 1981, 179–183). The fact that "these concepts are tacitly construed by Moroccans as Islamic, if not human, universals, makes their resulting vision of the world all the more reasonable and compelling" (1976, 125).

The congruence between Islam's "common-sense perspective" and the "prevailing everyday orientation toward social reality" (Eickelman 1976, 153) ensconces religious belief as a legitimizing agent in social change. Yet the faith's adaptiveness goes beyond several key Islamic concepts. Specifically, the rural-based religious orientation "consists of a flexible reservoir of meaning which rests on a base of widely differing elements: symbols, rituals, actions, formalized language, powerful emotions, concepts, parables, notions. The elements are derived from a variety of sources—the universal faith, the culture, the social world, the individual believer" (Combs-Schilling 1982, 14). Additionally, the religious orientation "is not clearly bounded. New elements are incorporated. Old ones lie fallow and still others are revitalized as the orientation changes over time. Any one of the elements can serve as focal point of stability and kingpin of the faith while others change" (Combs-Schilling 1982, 15). The many elements constituting the religious orientation are not themselves

> formalized and systematized into a coherent conceptual whole. They are not integrated into an ideology. . . . Since the elements of religious orientation are not rigorously systematized, they need not be deductively related. People can hold beliefs that appear from a logical standpoint contradictory. . . . A consequence of the lack of systematization is that individual

elements can be used pragmatically and situationally without calling the system as a whole into question. Religious orientation is not some abstract coherent system that, when confronted with information it cannot integrate, cracks and leaves people without a means of support. On the contrary, it is a flexible resource base (Combs-Schilling 1982, 16).

What all this means for Moroccans is that the reality of Islamic practice is one of synthesis and accommodation rather than one of mutual exclusivity. "Taken together in various syntheses according to temporal and social contexts, the [faith's multiple] conceptions have enabled Islam to encompass many varieties of social experience and to be regarded at any given time as a meaningful religious representation of reality" (Eickelman 1976, 12). Viewed this way, Islam becomes a powerful legitimizing instrument for mediating change.

In summary:

> Islam is a power in Morocco. Its strength comes from the faith itself and from the flexibility of the religious orientation through which that faith is expressed. Islam's public and private usefulness derives from the variety of elements which comprise it, the variety of means through which they are apprehended, and the flexibility with which they are applied. Islam is situationally adaptable, personally meaningful and yet laden with universal truth. Islam is diverse, changing, and private, and yet unified, stable and universal. A certainty is its potency. It remains a resource upon which king, counselor and beggar rely (Combs-Schilling 1982, 31).

MOROCCAN ISLAM

Islam in Morocco, as elsewhere in North Africa, assumes different organizational forms however much the central tenets of the faith remain the same. Three categories of Islamic expression manifest themselves in contemporary Morocco: saintly, scripturalist, and social.

The saintly or maraboutic tradition is more important for the "Morocco that was" than for the "Morocco that is," although its "sentimental authority" still exists today (Geertz 1968, 44). Believers in and supporters of marabouts—saintly persons possessed of *baraka*, or blessedness—in Morocco see them and other saints, mystics, and holy men, "as a hierarchy of intermediaries through whom the supernatural pervades, sustains, and affects the universe." For the rural folk and those elsewhere who subscribe to such beliefs, these "intermediaries with God are part of Islam as they understand it." From their perspectives "they regard themselves as Muslims, pure and simple" and not believers of an "amalgam of Islamic and non-Islamic elements" (Eickelman 1976, 10).

In Morocco's past, marabouts enjoyed exceptional prestige and power in the religious, political, and economic worlds. Through their simple, emotional, and popular rituals, marabouts had particular appeal among the plain country folk, whose lack of education made it difficult for them to assimilate the Koranic teachings and dogma practiced by the orthodox Islamic clergy and *ulama* (religious-legal scholars) in the cities. Indeed, much of maraboutism's populist appeal was in direct reaction to the aridity of orthodox Islam and the moribund schools of Islamic theology patronized by the religious legal scholars.

Essentially intuitive and transcendental in their theology, the marabouts, stressing community solidarity, mutual assistance, and self-defense, offered psychological reinforcement to the masses who followed them in a way that the mosques, schools, and courts could not.

Their popularity and significance in the organization of religious life in the countryside had wide political and social implications: Marabouts became important community figures, acting in various roles such as tribal leader, arbitrator in family and clan disputes, businessman. Eventually maraboutic brotherhoods emerged, constituting a kind of corporate institutionalization of folk religion. During its peak period between the fifteenth and midseventeenth centuries, maraboutism functioned as a vast rural revivalist cause. Beyond the control of whatever putative central authority existed in urban centers, the religious brotherhoods, whose legitimacy was enhanced by religious sanction, served real organizational and social functions.

In the modern period, marabouts have lost much of their political and social significance. "Most have no following outside their immediate localities and restricted influence even within their home districts" (Tessler 1982, 59). The government neither encourages nor discourages maraboutic cults but instead views them as a symptom of a vigorous folk culture. Nonetheless, for many Western-trained anthropologists, "maraboutism continues to hold its ground among the majority of the population" (Eickelman 1976, 236). Collectively these investigators report "that many rural individuals have strong personal ties to Sufi orders and other religious institutions, that socializing in the context of worship at brotherhood lodges often fosters important political and economic relationships, that popular religious figures are still highly esteemed by some segments of the rural population, and that religious ties and piety are often factors in local prestige, enhancing an individual's status and perceived fitness for leadership" (Tessler 1982, 59; see also Eickelman 1976; Dwyer 1978a; and Maher 1974).

What is beyond debate, however, is the relationship of maraboutism to the Muslim consensus in general and the monarchy in particular—maraboutism strongly supports both regardless of the "un-Islamic" character of its beliefs and practices. For many pious people in the countryside, King Hassan is the "supreme marabout," who possesses *baraka* to a superlative degree. Indeed, with the extremely strong support that the rural bourgeoisie, at the elite level, and the practitioners of mysticism, at the mass level, show for king and throne, the historic division between *makhzan* and *siba* has been inverted. Now it is the countryside that is firmly behind the government while the cities are the source of challenge to central authority.

Scripturalism constitutes "official," "formal," or "reformist" Islam, which is propagated by the monarchy, the *ulama*, reformist Muslims, and other religious spokesmen located in the society's modern, urban centers but having national influence. As protectors of orthodox Islam, scripturalists reject maraboutism completely. Yet, like their saintly counterparts, the *ulama* buttress the Muslim consensus and are an integral part of the monarchical

TABLE 2.1 Scripturalist and Saintly Islam

Scripturalist, Official, Reformist, Orthodox Islam	Saintly, Folk, Maraboutic Islam
1. Puritanical, based on strict conformity to rules of Islam as elaborated in the Koran, hadiths, and sharia	1. No relationship to Koran, hadiths, and formal Islamic law
2. Religion of urban elites with education	2. Religion of the illiterate masses
3. Emphasizes unmediated relationship between God and man	3. Saints as mediators between God and man
4. Monotheistic	4. Worship of saints
5. Egalitarian	5. Hierarchical; patrilineal descendant of Prophet and prominent saints having higher status than everyone else
6. Sober and rational	6. Ritual indulgences associated with shrines of saints and Sufi mysticism

system, to which they provide religious legitimacy of an institutional nature. Both king and orthodox clergy need each other. This is not to suggest that the latter are "lackeys" to the throne, for as "protectors of Islam and the welfare of Muslims" (Tessler 1982, 59), they are in a position to speak authoritatively on matters relating to the faith.

For a summary of the differing orientations of saintly and scripturalist Islam see Table 2.1 (see Munson 1984, 25; Geertz 1968, 9; and Gellner 1969, 7–8). The dichotomy represented in Table 2.1 is not so sharp in the minds of most Moroccan faithful as it is among religious "professionals" and those involved in articulating a distinctive religious message. Scripturalist and saintly Islam are not so far apart as assumed by anthropologists when they elaborate on the key domains of the believers' own perception of the faith and the ways that religious symbols are used in ritual and everyday life. As indicated earlier, the reality of Islamic practice in Morocco is one of fusion rather than of two separate, adversary (sub)faiths.

The same cannot be said of "social" or populist Islam as represented by revivalist or fundamentalist Muslim movements that have arisen recently in Morocco, as in other parts of the Arab-Islamic world. Inasmuch as the *intégriste*, or fundamentalist, thrust in Morocco will be treated more fully later, only a brief sketch will be provided here. While rooted in the same basic worldview and ethos as scripturalist, and to a lesser extent, saintly, Islam, social Islam is much more revolutionary, authoritarian, action oriented, and globalist in its interpretation of the faith and the determination of what constitutes proper conduct and behavior for the believer. Religious devoutness and ritual practice are not enough: Direct, total, and absolute political and social action is required on a global scale. This ideological dimension of militant Islam sets it apart, in clear and dramatic terms, from its competitors. Specifically, Muslim activists "invoke a revaluation of the role of Islam in society and question the secularization of cultural life, social practices antithetical to Islamic precepts, and the implementation of positivist law. Especially condemnable is the influence of Western society, held responsible for having carried Muslim society far from the basic tenets of organic Islam" (Waltz 1986, 651).

Supported mainly by the young and the alienated, the "new" Islam seeks many things: "a purification of values and behavior among [the faithful] and an assault on what [is] perceived as Western libertarianism and atheism (Marxist or capitalist); a social revolution, an attack on private property; the redistribution of wealth in the society. All share in the ideal of physical sacrifice for their cause; a willingness to resort to violence and a general feeling that the regimes under which they live have become corrupt beyond salvage" (Waterbury 1982).

As we shall see later, the impact of revivalist Islam has been weakest in Morocco, in contrast to the threat it poses for Algerian and Tunisian secular authorities. One of the revolutionary dimensions of militant Islam, for example, is to try to rupture the national-religious symbiosis that most Arab regimes have been working under since independence. Specifically, the fundamentalists argue that loyalty should only be to the *umma* (the community of Muslim believers) and not shared with loyalty to the *watan* (nation) inasmuch as the latter is an "artificial" concept introduced and imposed by the West on the Arabs. In Morocco, however, the *umma-watan* distinction does not apply because government symbols, institutions, and practices are designed to reinforce the religious and secular legitimacy of the state with which the overwhelming majority identify. As long as the Muslim consensus remains at the core of Moroccan efforts at modernization and development, radical appeals for fidelity to religious community but not nation find little receptivity. To be sure, many Moroccans are sympathetic to the grievances articulated by Muslim militants—corruption, nepotism, injustice—but most reject their solutions along with their tactics. Nonetheless, Muslim fundamentalists will continue to call for the "re-Islamization" of society while attacking Morocco's secular elites but, revealingly, not the king or the monarchy.

Chapter Three

Culture
and Politics

The overwhelming majority of Moroccans are indifferent to but not ignorant of politics. Indeed, for most, "politics" is either irrelevant or insignificant. For those at the top as well as those at the bottom, personal relations, family ties, tribal affiliations, and clientelist networks are what count. Political elites use modern instrumentalities—political parties, trade unions, mass media—in pursuit of traditional (personalistic and primordially oriented) goals. People at the bottom do not have the necessary skills or resources to expand their "choices." Yet for both categories, politics as a system of compromise, give-and-take, and collective effort to achieve commonly accepted national goals is only dimly understood or appreciated, and rarely applied.

In such a milieu it really matters little if the majority of Moroccans identify with or support the king as long as they lack the instruments to act autonomously on behalf of that support. A very small number of well-equipped army officers representing no one but themselves could manage to overthrow the monarchy, despite the broad base of "support" the king might have among most ordinary people.

The only national-level identity-forming issues that *all* participants in the system must uphold, however manipulatively, are the three pillars of the Muslim consensus—Islam, Arabism, and Moroccan nationalism. Beyond this cultural "core" everything is up for grabs. That is why the three (sub)cultural orientations—modernist, militarist, messianic—could easily become counter-cultures and regardless of the amount of support that each tendency commands, could, by either good luck or good planning, overthrow the monarchical system. Together this means that even in 1989 Moroccans do not yet recognize national-level politics as the means by which to rectify mistakes, attend to grievances, or respond to perceived injustices; for that they turn to *zaim* (notable), sharif, marabout, or local authority and power. In brief, for the majority of Moroccans, culture does not yet relate in any direct way to national-level politics except in the symbol of the king. Culture changes slowly and remains relatively unresponsive to explicitly "modern" political groupings, practices, and expectations. An explanation of this phenomenon follows.

COGNITIVE DIMENSION: STRUCTURAL AND SUBSTANTIVE

Morocco is a "political" society in the sense that "who gets what, when, and how" is the preoccupation of so many men (and far fewer women) in their daily discussions, whether at home or at work, in coffeehouses or social clubs, in the city or in the countryside. The country's strong oral tradition has long been a great source of information, gossip, and hearsay about what everyone else is doing or thought to be doing, including those involved in political machinations at the very top. With modern education and constant travel within and without the country, often related to migratory labor patterns and advanced telecommunications systems, this "knowledgeability" factor has increased manyfold. Attitudinal surveys of elementary school-children in Casablanca, Marrakesh, and Rabat, for example, reveal an early acquisition of political information and knowledge (Suleiman 1985). In short, historical tradition combined with observational and attitudinal data all confirm a high level of political understanding among Moroccan men and among the educated of both sexes. Yet the statement of one ordinary Moroccan that "no man with a brain in his head gets involved in politics in Morocco" (Munson 1984, 13) captures the essential contradiction of culture and politics in the country. For the majority of average Moroccans, politics is viewed as a "dangerous and pointless activity that should be avoided at all cost" (Munson 1984, 13).

The elite-manipulated system of clientelist and patrimonial politics, which has for so long dominated Moroccan national and local politics and with which are associated all kinds of abuses, has resulted in a profound malaise at the mass level and cynicism, distrust, and disgust at the elite level. This is what makes militant Islam so potentially revolutionary a force; more than any other cultural orientation, militant Islam has excited the imagination of not simply elements of the sub- or incipient elite but, more importantly, militant Islam has aroused the participatory instincts of thousands of ordinary Moroccans to get directly involved in politics in a manner never before imagined. This important dimension of political counterculture will be treated in more detail later.

When it comes to political participation and involvement, especially at the national level, there is a "silent majority" in Morocco—"those persons or collectivities who do not actively participate in formal politics" (Eickelman 1986, 182). This term refers both to those who are "turned off" or totally indifferent to the system as well as to those who have been expressly excluded by political actors. For most Moroccans, politics is viewed as an instrument for self-aggrandizement by those involved in it and thus best avoided. In the 1980s the system itself has begun to respond more positively to public demands for authentic forms of political participation, but these limited instances have not yet been sufficiently internalized or widely accepted enough to constitute the basis of a new participatory political culture. This may yet develop if the current policy of incremental democratization is allowed to continue in the immediate future. But for now, Moroccans remain extremely distrustful, cynical, and suspicious of the manner in which national political life is conducted. Most of these attitudes derive from the way monarchical power has been (ab)used and manipulated since independence.

Everyone understands one thing about politics in Morocco: Personality overpowers organization. Power is not exercised through the formal channels of politics and authority, although in recent years established political structures and governmental institutions, particularly the multiparty system, have been revitalized and given a new sense of purpose and direction; power is exercised through a highly developed system of clientelism. The essential feature of such a patrimonial system is the basic patron-client relationship, involving the exchange of resources between key figures in government and strategically located individuals. In return for these resources, the government or head of state receives economic and political support. The emphasis is on the personal nature of the exchange; hence the alternate term, *personalism*. Tessler summarized this phenomenon in the case of Morocco in the following manner: "Political power is accumulated and exercised through participation in a system of political and economic clientelism, by being able to situate oneself in the upper levels of a series of intersecting networks of patron-client relationships" (1982, 63; see also Waterbury 1970). Clientelism is sustained by the use of existing elite contacts and connections to obtain access to resources that are then used both to advance one's self-interest and to create larger alliances and interdependencies.

As with the concept of tribal segmentation, Waterbury argued that clientelism and personalism in today's Morocco are continuations of long-established patterns. "An organization, the clientele party; a political function, arbitration; and a political role, zaim [inspiring leader] are recurring themes in Moroccan political style. All three have a long history in Morocco and have been adapted for use in the present political setting" (1970, 88).

Although many have predicted the eventual disappearance of this clientelist system as the educated population demanding greater participation in the system has increased, personalism, patrimonialism, and patron-client relations continue to prevail, both as political forms and as explanations of the power configuration in the state. The palace remains at the center of a whole patronage system upon which clientelism depends.

Explanations for the persistence of clientelism focus on the apparent continuing congruence between traditional Moroccan values relating to power and authority and the manner in which Moroccan elites direct political life. Although there is a clear relationship between society's traditional values and norms and the way political elites behave, one must be careful not to endow this association "with too much explanatory power" (Tessler 1982, 65). Segmentary tribal politics, clientelism, and other forms of traditional patrimonial behavior are not the only forces at work in the socialization of a national elite: modern education, secular life-styles, and Westernized social norms have also been influential. There is no doubt, however, that patron-client relations and "participation in a top heavy political machine" (Tessler 1982, 65) have displaced all other forms of politics in the state (Waterbury 1973a, 534). In brief, patron-client relations are the "mechanisms that organize elite interaction, and they define the behavioral norms according to which the elite seek to gain and exercise power" (Tessler 1982, 65).

The label "patrimonialism" seems inappropriate given the fact that, along with the system's person-centered power constellations, a modern, national institutionalized bureaucracy has developed. Indeed, according to one observer, the Moroccan monarchy is in transition from a patrimonialism founded on traditional forms of legitimacy to one of "contractual neopatrimonialism" involving the essential exchange of services among local elites and state elites (Waterbury 1979, 414).

This contractual neopatrimonialism still possesses all the attributes of patrimonialism—personalism, proximity, informality, balance of conflict, military prowess, and religious rationalization (see Bill and Leiden 1984, 159–176)—but now they are incorporated into the modern state system and are involved in administration, technology, and the military (Waterbury 1979, 412). These strong rationalizing tendencies in the neopatrimonial system possess two dimensions: a central bureaucracy that is increasingly subject to rational criteria of organization, recruitment, and training; and political elites that, in terms of education, exposure to outside currents of thought, mental outlook, and career expectations, are "somewhat" removed from the traditionalistic, clientelistic, and particularistic ethos of the patrimonial regime (Waterbury 1973a, 535).

These points notwithstanding, however, most of these changes in Moroccan political life have more to do with "form" and "style" than with the underlying base of legitimacy, which continues in large part to rest on Islam (Combs-Schilling 1982, 4). In other words, although "the organizational mechanics of the present bureaucracy tend to be phrased in lay terms, the religious and traditional idioms often are used to reinforce the bureaucratic links. Whatever the idiom of operational mechanics,

Morocco's political forms past and present have rested their ultimate legitimacy in Islam" (Combs-Schilling 1982, 5). On the one hand, this has enabled those controlling national politics to continue to communicate in the primordial idiom traditional people best understand, but on the other, it has alienated the more politically educated and alert segment of society who feel that although style has changed, substance has not. Surprisingly, these same modernist forces have not turned to secular ideology to counter (neo)patrimonial power.

There is no generally accepted system of political belief or ideology in Morocco. Heightened Islamic consciousness and identity with the Moroccan nation and its Arab component have not yet been formulated into explicit ideologies, though fundamentalist tendencies probably have the greatest potential for ideological formulation. The "Muslim consensus" defines a broadly agreed upon normative system of beliefs rather than a set of programmatic directives or institutional mechanisms intended to transform principles into practice. Instead, political elites subscribe to tacitly accepted norms and implicit preferences.

What passes for ideology is little more than a vague agreement on the necessity—even the desirability—of economic growth and a more equitable distribution of wealth. Even the notion of *civisme*, a blend of civic spirit and religious values, through which the king hoped to influence future citizens and subjects, has consisted of little more than patrimonial pedagogy and preaching. Yet even such "noble" sentiments as economic justice and civic virtue are compromised by a visible reluctance to make personal sacrifices for broader social goals. Elite political culture in Morocco is virtually devoid of a public service orientation; incumbents are concerned with preserving and, whenever possible, enhancing their personal positions. This deficient civic-mindedness of Moroccan society very much resembles the politics of patrimonialism long associated with the discredited Lebanese political system.

> The politically relevant members of [Moroccan] society are not inclined to allow the obligations, which arise from their membership in the society, to supervene when they feel that interests which they regard as vital are threatened. These

interests are the integrity of their communities of belief and
primordial attachment—of kinship and locality—and the opportunities and possessions of the constituent groups or individual members of these communities. Actions in the public
sphere of [Moroccan] society are assessed in too many situations
by their prospective consequences for the situation of these
communities of belief and primordial attachment (Shils 1966,
2).

Within the scheme of patron-client relations, pragmatism
prevails. Consequently political ideology, or any socioeconomic
equivalent, is shunned in favor of flexibility, with emphasis on
the greatest liberty to form and alter personal ties, where and
when they seem most appropriate and advantageous. This
attitude holds for urban bourgeoisie as well as for rural notables.
As Waterbury has indicated, politics for the typical rural notable,
although less so for his offspring, is

> devoid of ideological content. He reduces everything to the
> simplest acts of power. He conceives of political organizations
> as neutral receptacles which can be filled, occupied and vacated
> by any imaginable combination of compatriots. A political
> party, a resistance group, or a union are but enlarged alliance
> systems, ready-made so to speak, membership in which implies
> no commitment to a program, ideology or set of goals, but
> rather furnishes the adherent with allies to whom he is obligated
> and who are in turn obligated to him (Waterbury 1970, 117).

In short, for political elites in the countryside and in the cities,
Moroccan political parties are viewed as nothing more than
"open-ended receptacles devoid of ideological content" (Waterbury 1970, 118). Although there is preliminary evidence that
parties are being reanimated within a more authentically pluralistic political system (see Zartman 1985), elite attitudes and
behavior still reflect the primacy of personalism over ideology.
    At the mass level, widespread apathy and cynicism prevail.
For most ordinary Moroccan men and women, neither ideology
nor political organization provides the most effective instrument
for overcoming perceived grievances. This situation is accurately
captured in the individual portrayals of a Muslim fundamentalist

male and a Muslim Westernized female as described by Munson (1984). In a vague and unsystematic way, the fundamentalist male, al-Hajj Muhammed, saw fundamentalism, not secular ideology, as the appropriate response to perceived disparities in wealth (socioeconomic grievance), the foreign domination of the Moroccan economy (nationalist grievance), and the dilution of the purity of the faith by the adoption and use of Christian cultural ways (religious grievance) (Munson 1984, 4). The Westernized female (Fatima Zohra) saw these problems in essentially the same light but responded in totally different ways; for her, solutions were phrased in secular terms. Although she also complained about "foreign domination," her grievances centered more on the subordination of women in Moroccan society. In both instances, however, neither the fundamentalist male nor the secular female showed a commitment to a specific ideology or political organization. In short, there was no sense that perceived discontent will lead to committed action. These dual portrayals very much captured the generalized feeling extant among the majority of ordinary Moroccans that political ideology and political organization are the inappropriate responses to perceived conditions of socioeconomic or personal discontent.

This same phenomenon seems to apply to another category of Moroccan social types—the slum dweller. He too, like his fellow urban and rural citizens at the top as well as those of humbler standing, does not ordinarily turn to "rationalistic" ideology or organization as the means by which to resolve his many problems. The bidonvilles of Morocco are "the receptacles for migrants to the cities, and, as the dwelling-place of thousands of displaced, unemployed individuals, have been cited as a breeding ground of likely recruits for [secular] radical political movements [particularly of the left.] Implicit in this assumption [is] that the denizens of the bidonvilles constitute a proletariat in the European sense of the word" (Waterbury 1970, 200). This is not the case in Morocco. By extension, such symbols of rural ferment as rural exodus, unemployment, and bidonvilles are not the exclusive products of the impact of colonization and the process of modernization. These latter two phenomena accentuated and aggravated what was already going on. From the slums come petty criminals, hooligans, and misfits, not social revolutionaries of the left-wing variety. What revolutionary potential does exist in this milieu is attracted to Islamic fundamentalism; yet even that appeal tends to be as much opportunistic as ideological.

In a more positive light, many of the inhabitants of Casablanca's slums, for example, are not revolutionaries or criminals or social rebels. They eke out an existence but continue to maintain ties with the rural communities from which they originally came. Though fragile, these links with the traditional world are seldom broken. "Despite constant contact with industrial society and modern urban culture the impact on the behavior of the individual migrant, as well as upon his community of origin with which he is in frequent contact, has been [and remains] remarkably light. He does not break definitively with his upbringing, his childhood period of socialization, nor does he totally reject or defect from his rural culture" (Waterbury 1970, 202).

The continuity with the social past is not without political significance for the inhabitant of the bidonville. He is not the political radical, the alienated proletarian that some would see in him. "In fact he may be politically docile, or, if not, he rejects authority in ways common to the rural world" (Waterbury 1970, 202). Certainly he is capable of violence and protest as the riots in 1965, 1977, 1981, and 1984 amply demonstrated, "but his protests [are] brief, unguided, and formless. He is not a man with nothing to lose. The bidonville is more attractive to him than the bled" (Waterbury 1970, 202).

In combination, elite and mass attitudes reaffirm the primacy of the traditional over the ideological. Despite the many changes that have taken place in society and the economy, there is still a very low sense of civic purpose evident in Morocco. Shared values of economic self-interest rather than support for clearly identifiable ideological principles tend to characterize Moroccan political behavior. Those looking for "dramatic" changes in political ideas and behavior will be disappointed. Moroccan history has repeatedly demonstrated that changes take place gradually, incrementally, and in stages, but that changes take place nonetheless. Thus it remains doubtful that "the salience of ideological commitment and technical competence seem destined to rise in the long run, at the expense of family and political connections and of skill in building patron-client relationships" (Tessler 1982, 74). Despite the modern veneer—parties, parliament, unions, elections—in the final analysis, politics in Morocco can only be comprehended by appreciating the durability of nonrational patterns of behavior (Waterbury 1970, 92). Politicians, despite their Western appearances, education, multilingual proficiency, and other signs of European identity, continuously and instinctively demonstrate traditionally based forms of behavior. They thus continue to use power for defense, seek to establish debt relations, maneuver to create alliances, and always feel most comfortable in a situation of equilibrium. In this sense "there has been no clean break with the past" (Waterbury 1970, 92–93).

Incrementalism as a policy for achieving social and economic change under the label of adaptive modernization seems a prudent and sensible approach in the context of Moroccan history and traditional practices. The Moroccan approach seems appropriate compared to the alternative models available, such as those followed by various countries including prerevolutionary Iran, Algeria, Tunisia, Libya, and Egypt, each of which has experienced various levels of social upheaval and political turmoil.

In the political sphere, however, incrementalism's appropriateness has become problematic. Is it realistic to expect modern, rationalistic instruments of governance and administration, including modern bureaucracies, armies, scientific and educational institutions, and business enterprises, to function effectively, productively, and responsibly in a cultural environment so permeated by traditional values? As already pointed out, the absence of comprehensive ideological parties, genuinely free of royal manipulation, has left a legacy of apathy and cynicism among elite and nonelite alike. If incremental democratization is to have any real meaning, political power must begin to respond rationally, predictably, and equitably to the myriad demands that society makes on its political system.

As an adaptive patrimonial system, Morocco has strong rationalizing tendencies—there is the adoption of technical innovation, scientific education, and economic enterprise—but political power remains centralized in a traditional structure, the hereditary monarchy. Although fundamental traditional norms have not changed and, in some cases, are being further ensconced in society, there have been intermittent attempts to allow politics and administration to operate under more "neutral" and achievement-oriented criteria. The 1984 national legislative elections, for example, were conducted along relatively democratic lines with less than usual government interference, fraud, and intimidation. Yet for most Moroccans this experience is still too recent, too inconclusive, and preceded by too many instances of such experiments coming to nought to have transformed political culture and political attitudes. Thus in terms of the substantive aspect of political cognition, the view remains prevalent that power and politics are the monopoly of the few, that political institutions are rather insignificant, and that government service is an opportunity to advance private and family interests, not to work for the betterment of society as a whole.

The many instances of real or alleged corruption, fraud, and mismanagement in high places simply confirm this basic view of men in authority. Indeed, abuses have gotten so out of hand during King Hassan's rule that corruption is no longer considered simply an aspect of politics but has virtually "displaced and dwarfed all other forms of politics" (Waterbury 1973a, 534; see also Gillespie and Okruhlik 1988, 73). Rather than being considered an unfortunate deviancy in an otherwise honest attempt at conducting better government, free-floating corruption is manipulated, guided, planned, and "desired" by the regime itself. These, then, are not instances of petty graft and bribery characteristic of many Third World systems in which inefficient bureaucracies can be maintained only through low-level chronic corruption. In Morocco, corruption is at the heart of the political system, which itself is dominated by the king. Corruption, defined as the "sharing of the spoils available through the linkage of the traditional patronage system with modern administrative system," is seen as the basic element of control used by the king, who sits atop both systems (Nelson 1978, 222–223).

Regardless of the extent, type, or frequency of corrupt practices in the state, Moroccan politics are dominated by the patronage system with the king in almost complete control of the "great patronage machine" from which he gains much of his power (Waterbury 1973a, 554).

The way the king maintains his control over the political system can be seen with specific regard to the civil service. The king explicitly encourages a sense of career instability, which, although it may lead to policy impotence, nonetheless ensures the king's royal authority. Most Moroccan bureaucrats at the level of *chef de service* (department head) and above are at the mercy of the discretionary powers of promotion, transfer, and retention vested in the minister, who is himself directly appointed by and personally responsible to the king himself. To date, no institutional defense exists that can protect the always vulnerable bureaucrat from the whims and temperaments of the king. The only "compensation" offered to participants in this political process is access to the spoils system. "Access is subject to the arbitrary manipulation of the Palace, and hence is supportive of patrimonial ties" (Waterbury 1973a, 553).

Very few Moroccans have any illusions about how this system operates or who controls it, "certainly not the king or the participants, nor, for the most part, the masses. There is a general level of cynicism running throughout—the cynicism of the nonparticipant masses who fall back on the traditional reflex, 'government has ever been thus'; the cynicism of the participants who partake of the system individually while refusing any responsibility for it; and the cynicism of the king who plays on the weakness and greed of his subjects" (Waterbury 1973a, 555).

Anywhere else in the Afro-Arab world, such deep and widespread feelings of personal cynicism would, in time, find expression in protest movements or other forms of oppositional sentiment, as happened, for example, in prerevolutionary Iran. But unlike the shah, who blatantly violated Iran's most cherished cultural traditions and symbols in the name of some alien, Western ideal, Morocco's monarchs have been exceptionally skillful in promoting the kinds of religious and traditional symbols with which the majority of Moroccans have a deep and direct association. Symbolic politics has been developed into a high art form in Morocco.

That the monarchy came to represent the heart of the Moroccan political and religious system was itself partially an accident of history. Most analysts agree that left to itself, the preindependence sultanate would have withered away or been superseded by the nationalist political parties that led the fight for independence. French colonial insensitivity and/or stupidity, in the manner in which it treated the sultan personally (he was imprisoned) and the sultanate institutionally (it was expressly bypassed), almost guaranteed that nationalist sentiment would crystallize around man and throne. Indeed, French maltreatment of the sultan so aroused Moroccan passions and mobilized popular feeling that "there is probably no other liberated colony in which the struggle for independence so centered around the capture, revival, and renovation of a traditional institution" (Geertz 1968, 78). This was best expressed in the inscriptions that appeared on the banners in the many nationalist demonstrations that swept the country in the immediate preindependence period: "Long live Islam!" "Long live Morocco!" "Long live the Sultan!" (Geertz 1968, 81).

When he became king at independence in 1956, Mohamed V was unlike any Moroccan monarch before him, an authentic popular hero. As Geertz correctly emphasized, "[it is unlikely] that there is any other new nation . . . in which the hero-leader of the revolution and independence was engulfed in *religious* authority, over and above the political, as Muhammed V was in Morocco in 1956" (1968, 81). Added to this, however, was the personality of the king himself, for he seems actually to have been a man of deep and genuine piety, which greatly enhanced both his popular appeal as a political leader and his charismatic attraction as the head of a religious community. From this populist base, symbolic politics assumed its central role in the state and from there King Hassan II, lacking the intrinsic charisma of his father, developed symbolic politics to an even more elaborate degree.

The monarch rests his power on several foundations: institutional, military, and religious, but Islam serves as the ultimate legitimator. Hassan has been adept at utilizing the full range of religious symbols to legitimize his regime. No ritual or symbol is taken for granted. This is best seen in the pomp and circumstance surrounding any appearance of the king, especially at an important function, whether religious (sacrificing the first ram on Aid el Kebir), cultural (inaugurating the tomb of Mohamed V), or political (visiting El Ayoun in the Western Sahara in March 1985). On such occasions the king, dressed in his white *jallaba* and shaded by his parasol, receives the homage of the ministers and high public officials, who kiss his hand as he passes on his horse (Waterbury 1979, 413).

During Islam's high holy days, the king's religious role assumes particular significance. Then, more than at any other time, the king serves as a center of the faith, which itself serves as the center of the polity. In every religiously related ritual during Ramadan, for example, the king's actions are given wide public attention on television, radio, and in the newspapers. During the holy month of fasting and introspection the king "appears nightly with the nation's official religious leaders and gives televised religious lessons himself. His command of formal Arabic, itself an important popular symbol of religious authority, is regarded as the best of any contemporary Arab leader, and his public image is constantly associated with the nation's religious and material welfare" (Eickelman 1986, 183). At no point in Ramadan's daily rituals is the king absent from public view: He is shown regularly at the mosque in prayer; he is at the very center of end-of-the-month festivities of breaking the fast (Aid es Seghir); on the Night of Revelation, Hassan is televised chanting the Koran; and during Ashura (alms giving to the poor), the king "makes widely publicized gifts to Morocco's poorer, and often more rebellious, regions" (Combs-Schilling 1982, 3). Hassan is carefully attentive to the symbols associated with his roles as civilian leader, military commander in chief, and religious head.

This is nowhere better demonstrated than in the king's clothing. During normal working days, the king wears Western-style suits, intended to reflect his modern orientation. For official celebrations and national events, Hassan dons a military uniform, representing his temporal power. During important and prestigious events, the king wears the elegant white robes of the hajj, as symbols of purity, equality, and Islam itself (Combs-Schilling 1982, 2). Increasingly, these white robes have become the king's sartorial trademark, for he wears them during his numerous public speeches, when he attends the televised mosque services, and when he receives the country's important religious figures at the palace. Additionally, Hassan "cloaks himself in the white robes for a number of ceremonies of state, for instance, the investiture of new ministers, the reception of Muslim foreign ambassadors" (Combs-Schilling 1982, 2).

In these and scores of other instances, the king has a virtual monopoly over the country's religious as well as nationalist symbols. Both are often combined, as in the case of Hassan's 1979 designation as president of the Committee on Jerusalem. In that capacity the Moroccan monarch was charged with the task of drawing international attention to the "Zionist occupation and desecration" of Islam's holy city as well as to mobilize worldwide Christian support for this leading Muslim cause. It is in such high-visibility positions where the king scores many symbolic "points" that cannot easily be duplicated or challenged by other groups or individuals in the society (see Tozy 1979).

The most dramatic and successful instance in which religious-nationalist-military symbols have been fused for purposes of enhancing legitimacy has been the king's policy in the Western Sahara (see Leveau 1985). Whatever else others outside of Morocco may think of this policy or the diplomatic defeats associated with it, the Western Sahara issue has galvanized nationalist pride and identity unlike anything since independence. The Green March of November 1975, for example, which saw nearly a half million Moroccan citizens mobilized on behalf of the "reintegration" of a portion of Morocco's "homeland," has been an immensely popular act that has seen virtually all sectors of society come together in support of the king's initiative. It has been an exceptionally important symbolic event, reuniting the Alawite dynasty with the history of the nation and its Islamic sources (Waterbury 1979, 417). As Miller has correctly observed: "[T]he drama and meaning of the Green March have emerged as a pivotal point in Moroccan nationhood and a powerful exercise in national consciousness" (1984, 189).

One can never know fully how these religiously inspired or politically motivated ritual acts are accepted by the mass of Moroccans. One can only speculate. A safe conclusion is that the overwhelming majority of rural folk, both bourgeois and peasant, and many of the lower classes in the city fully accept the religious rationalization of the monarchy. For them "Hassan is an impeccable Muslim" (Tessler 1982, 68). Deep doubts, however, exist among university-educated individuals at both extremes of the political spectrum—fundamentalists on the right, Marxists on the left—who believe the king feigns religiosity for political advantage. Among the non-Westernized masses, however, the royal household is both legitimate and mystical, feeding into the duality that continues to characterize cultural identity: the rational and the mystical, the here and now and the hereafter (see Waterbury 1979, 414).

In any case, none of these examples should be interpreted as merely the king's adept use of symbols in order to manipulate a gullible, sheeplike citizenry, a point of view often advanced by cynical urban intellectuals, opposition political leaders, and disgruntled religious figures. The authenticity and efficacy of symbolic politics in Morocco is nowhere better demonstrated than in an event loaded with potentially negative public image consequences: the celebration associated with a royal wedding.

The lavish splendor and spectacle surrounding the marriage of King Hassan's daughter, Laila Meriem, in mid-September 1984, did not seem out of place in a country still suffering from economic dislocations, poverty, and social disparities. While the public festivities associated with the wedding were shown on national television, there were few people who complained or criticized the events as being too excessive. "We expect our kings to still live like kings," was the comment of one middle-aged engineer (Schumacher 1984). In an interview at that time, the king was quoted as saying, "It's not my ceremony, but a ceremony for all Moroccans" (Schumacher 1984). As self-serving as that might sound, there is much truth to it. Once known for his playboy ways and dissolute life-style, King Hassan has been carefully cultivating for a number of years his image as a "traditional" Arab monarch. As already noted, in almost all his daily activities the king plays to tradition to enhance his popularity and legitimacy. Simultaneously and equally important has been his vanguard role in modernizing the country. Besides promoting education and technology, the king is now taking the lead in advancing a limited form of political evolution. Parliament does serve as a forum for political debate, albeit not political decisions, and the press is exceptionally free by African and Arab standards.

The king's policies of cultural synthesis, adaptive modernization, and incremental democratization are very much congruent with the medieval and modern sentiments that Moroccans as a whole have managed to blend effortlessly. As a noted U.S.-educated Moroccan sociologist teaching at the nation's premier university in Rabat has indicated, "There is no schizophrenia here" (Schumacher 1984). Like their monarch, Moroccan men and women of all classes and ages switch daily between wearing *jellabas* and *gandouras* and Western clothes. In the Moroccan context these outward symbols reflect more than just sartorial preferences: They reveal a level of cultural adaptiveness virtually absent elsewhere in the Arab world. Clearly the strong sense of national identity gives Moroccans the security to assimilate change without feeling threatened.

The degree to which society's integrative culture applies to a broad range of people and personalities is well illustrated in the case of Said Aouita—Morocco's sports hero who has become a symbol of athletic accomplishment and national pride. Although Aouita does not represent all lower-class Moroccans, he is typical of many large groups of people in the country—the partially urbanized, partially educated, "simple" individual struggling daily to eke out a respectable existence for himself and his family. If there is such a thing as a mass public orientation, the beliefs and behavior of Aouita come closest to representing it.

It is no exaggeration to say that in Morocco today runners have become national heroes. As an Olympic champion and world-record holder, Said Aouita has brought glory to Morocco: such glory that King Hassan has honored him as a symbol of his country's pride and hope. These sentiments cannot be underestimated in a society so very much moved by symbols, gestures, and rituals. In 1984 Aouita won the gold medal in the 5,000-meter race at the Los Angeles Olympics—the only gold medal won by an African male. A year later he set two world records (1,500 and 5,000 meters) and maintained that incredible pace in 1986 and 1987. What motivates this "ordinary" man? "It's not money or fame," he has said. "But I am a symbol for my people, especially the young ones. They can see that if I, one of the many, was able to make it, then they can too. I run for them" (Masback 1986, 30).

Currently among Aouita's many projects is the building of a sports stadium on land given to him by the king. This project combines all Aouita's loves: "athletics, music, helping others, and serving *his* King" (Masback 1986, 30) (emphasis added). He seems a man driven to succeed, guided by an individualistic ethic of hard work and perseverance, with which many Americans can identify. But there is a strong affective component as well that keeps him going. His drive for excellence comes "from the heart—from my love of sport and my love of my country," he has told interviewers (Masback 1986, 83).

Aouita was greatly moved when he received the Chevalier de l'Ordre du Trône, Morocco's highest honor, previously reserved to visiting heads of state; he was the first athlete to receive it. "When the King gave me the Chevalier, he took me in his arms like a son. That gesture meant more to me than the house or land he gave me. It shows the love of the King for his people and gives a sign of great hope to the young people of Morocco— 'You can do it too' he was telling them" (Masback 1986, 83). These words may sound naive and innocent to the hardheaded sophisticates of Casablanca and Rabat, but it is a sentiment strongly felt by many Moroccans to which the king is fully atuned and directly responsive.

On a slightly lower scale, but with potentially more profound social and cultural implications, are the athletic successes of another Moroccan track star—a woman. Nawal Moutawakil is a U.S.-trained athlete who won the 400-meter women's hurdle at the 1984 Olympics and became the first African or Arab woman ever to achieve such a distinction. All Moroccan women felt proud and honored by this achievement. As Fatima Mernissi has explained: "Nawal is not an exception, but a movement" (Schumacher 1984).

Unlike women in most of the Arab world, Moroccan females have moved into top jobs in universities, hospitals, government ministries, and the liberal professions. In many ways the accomplishments of Moroccan women, however modest by U.S. standards, give concrete meaning to the monarchy's pursuit of synthesis, adaptiveness, and incrementalism as the formula for development. To be sure, a culture of male domination prevails in Morocco, as elsewhere in the Arab-Islamic world, with all the negative consequences this has for female emancipation, integrity, and equality (see Dwyer 1978a; Maher 1974, 1978; Mernissi 1975, 1987; Rassam 1980; and Davis 1978). Additionally, existing family laws and other legislation pertaining to male-female relations perpetuate a cultural ideology of female sexual inferiority. For some feminists, "the seventh century concept of sexuality, as embodied in the modern family laws, conflicts dramatically with the sexual equality and desegregation fostered by modernization" (Mernissi 1975, xx). From the point of view of the most Westernized and liberated of Morocco's intellectual females, such as sociologist Mernissi, the Muslim consensus is but an ideological rationalization intended to subjugate females further and maintain male political hegemony.

One must be cautious, however, in applying too literally or directly cultural conditions of one society (the United States) to an altogether different one (Morocco). Certainly inequality, seg-regation, and discrimination in male-female relations are social realities in Morocco today. Yet the monarchical approach of adapting the old to fit the new has probably advanced more in Morocco as it applies to feminist issues than anywhere else in the Arab-Islamic world. In Morocco's largest cities, for example, women have made significant progress in many fields of endeavor, including regional and local politics. Although no woman cur-rently sits in the parliament or in the cabinet, Moroccan females are not without power and influence. In a study analyzing leading women's organizations, elite women's political partici-pation in and out of government, and women's major concerns, one author concluded that although women were not at the highest level of political authority in the state, they were very much evident in national bureaucracies and subministerial po-sitions, especially in matters relating to social affairs. "Even these mid-level and lower level [female] bureaucrats perform a crucial function in data gathering for and implementing policies" (Howard-Merriam 1984, 23). Similarly, a recent "survey of Moroccan employment patterns revealed that women constitute

29.9 percent of the liberal professions and scientific fields, and 27.7 percent of civil service employees" (Mernissi 1987, xxvii).

In summary, Morocco's cultural synthesis has provided extensive opportunities to many women, especially in the cities, for educational and career advancement. Women in Moroccan society are infinitely more "liberated," in virtually every sense of the word, than their sisters in neighboring "revolutionary" Algeria. With this said, however, the fact remains that Morocco is a male-centered society, that women in the rural areas remain dismally backward, and that political life at the top is the exclusive preserve of men. Although there are many instances of individual success stories, whether a Moutawakil or a Mernissi, women do not yet expresss their problems in collectivist terms. As long as Moroccan politics remains a "labyrinthine network of overlapping patron-client ties" (Eickelman 1986, 186), established by and for men, women will continue to have to struggle on their own. Fortunately, they at least do not confront the threat of losing what they have already gained as the result of fundamentalist pressures to enforce more traditionalist (read: sexist) laws and practices as they apply to women. The extensive backsliding on women's rights that has taken place throughout much of the Arab-Islamic world in recent years as a consequence of the rise of fundamentalist Islam has not happened in Morocco. Should current policies remain in force or be expanded, one can expect to see greater numbers of Moroccan women involved in politics, both as electors and as decisionmakers.

EVALUATIVE DIMENSION

Consistent with the many dualities and contradictions that characterize contemporary Moroccan society is the fact that Morocco is one of the very few Arab countries—pre-1975 Lebanon, post-Nasser Egypt, and independent Tunisia are the others—where opportunities exist for relatively unhampered social science research. One consequence has been the appearance of a plethora of attitudinal surveys, especially of university students, conducted by native and foreign researchers and scholarly investigators (see Moore 1970; Stone 1973; Suleiman 1985; Munson 1986; Tozy 1984; Etienne and Tozy 1979; Palmer and Nedelcovych 1984; Nedelcovych and Palmer 1982; Nedelcovych 1980; Moore and Hochschild 1968; Howard-Merriam 1984; Ashford 1961b, 1964; Waterbury 1973a; Selosse 1973; and Pascon and Bentahar 1972). Such a relatively large body of attitudinal research data has given investigators an opportunity to describe and analyze Moroccan cultural orientations in much greater depth and sophistication than is available, for example, in neighboring Algeria, where the research climate is hostile and therefore knowledge of its sociopsychological and cultural orientations very limited. In other words, these prefatory comments are intended to highlight the fact that one learns as much about Morocco from the very existence of an open research environment as from the diverse data that specific research projects produce. It is also intended as a cautionary note for those who might endow too much explanatory significance to such findings at the expense of appreciating the relatively pluralistic milieu in which they are generated. These caveats aside, how do Moroccans evaluate their political community, institutions, leaders, and policy outputs?

In the aggregate, students judge their political institutions and leaders harshly, criticize policy outputs as "too little, too late," yet strongly support the legitimacy and integrity of the Moroccan nation-state. Like the majority of Moroccans, students identify with the Muslim consensus but do not necessarily believe that the current political system is organized to promote and protect it. Whether on the ideological left or right, from privileged elite classes or humbler milieus, male or female, all students consistently criticize Moroccan politics. Public officials are held in extremely low regard for having compromised themselves to the "system" and its manipulative, corrupt ways. The idealism of youth combines with the cynicism of practical experience gained either directly through contact with the system or indirectly through the experiences of others to create an alienated, disaffected, and disenchanted Moroccan student population. One wonders whether this orientation has been so deeply ingrained from one generational cohort to another that it has become a permanent part of the youth-student subculture.

In any case, elite manipulation, administrative corruption, and governmental abuse provide ample evidence to arouse an already distrustful and cynical student community.

Whereas students on the left complain bitterly about a system intended to perpetuate elite economic and political privileges, those on the right attack the regime's insensitivity to cultural values and Islamic practices. Both groups are resentful about the way political power is abused to the advantage of the few. Whatever the current language of protest—Marxist in the 1950s and 1960s, Islamic fundamentalist in the 1970s and 1980s—in the minds of most students the basic problems of the country have not changed. Political alienation and disaffection are widespread. Most students believe that the system is insensitive to their own and the nation's needs and that "politics as usual" is the least effective way of producing change. The result is fairly low turnouts for elections, which are viewed in any case as managed and controlled by the palace with little real opportunity for autonomous political action. One report concluded, "Moroccan students [find] their political system to be unresponsive. They also [feel] almost totally hopeless in terms of attempting to alter it by what may be termed democratic means" (Palmer and Nedelcovych 1984, 120). In brief, university students—the group most vocal, most opinionated, and most surveyed in the country—have maintained a relatively constant negative view of political life for over twenty years.

This is not to say, however, that there has been no change. Earlier studies tended to report a much deeper level of discontent—"no survey can do justice to the resentment the average Moroccan student feels toward the regime" (Moore 1970, 291)—than is currently the case. For example, one recent study of secondary school students in Casablanca, Marrakesh, and Rabat reported fairly high levels of positive identification with and personal support of political institutions, symbols, and leaders (Suleiman 1985). Nonetheless, as other studies have shown, adult political socialization and experience tend to be much more determinative of enduring political beliefs and behavior than similar such experiences during childhood (Almond and Verba 1980). In other words, if past experience is any guide, the younger generational cohort will turn increasingly cynical, distrustful, and politically apathetic as its members come more directly into contact with the political system itself.

An important compensatory dimension to this basically negative evaluation of political system and process is the way the monarch and the monarchy are excluded from direct public attacks. As much as students and other youth criticize the elites in power and occasionally the institution of the monarchy, the person of the king is normally spared such abuse—at least in public. The contrast with the shah of Iran, who was so hated and vilified by the majority of students in and out of the country, is instructive in this regard. To be sure, Moroccan youth have consistently been skeptical about the monarchy. Many of them willingly submit "in order to be assured of sinecures in the lower ranks of the civil service or in the government-financed enterprises. Many maintain a careful neutrality while inwardly being resentful and discontented" (Ashford 1973, 105).

Many university students and young people in general are cowed, alienated, or repelled. Yet they dare not publicly diminish or demean the king who, for ordinary Moroccans, is the very symbol of Morocco itself; to do otherwise is to guarantee alienating the very mass public in whose name idealistic youth invoke their demands for a just social order. This leaves educated youth in a dilemma: The political system that they so abhor is at bottom controlled through the patrimonialism, patronage, and the political power of the monarch, but if they attack the king publicly and directly, such an act would alienate them from the populist base with which they would like to identify. This is in addition to, of course, the fear of government reprisal for those calling for the king's overthrow. This dilemma remains acute because, although changes are being introduced, there is still very little being done by the government in general and the king in particular "to give youth an image of government as an instrument of change within which each person can individually seek his role and make his contribution" (Ashford 1973, 105). Attitudinal surveys confirm this view of government indifference. Although students are politically aware and support in principle the idea of political participation, they remain extremely skeptical about the efficacy of utilizing existing political structures in an environment in which informal and personal ties are so pervasive (see Palmer and Nedelcovych 1984). Even though the political party system is presently being reinvigorated and has a potential of effectively distancing itself from the palace, it will take some time before this process has decisive impact on the way the youth of Morocco currently evaluate political life.

This situation is being further aggravated by the substantial socioeconomic problems that face all strata of Moroccan society but that have special significance for the partially and the inappropriately qualified. Job opportunities are few and competitive, income disparities and social inequalities are widening rapidly, overpopulation and overurbanization continue unchecked, and expectations run far ahead of state capabilities. Inevitably these multiple dilemmas are placed at the doorstep of the political system, which is then blamed for not producing satisfactory results. The riots of 1979, 1981, and 1984, for example, were very much associated with social frustrations stemming from underlying problems of inequality, unemployment, and poverty, along with a sense of political and social marginalization (see Seddon 1984, 11).

Students obviously do not constitute the largest or even the most critical segment of Moroccan society. Yet, unlike any other strategic group, save possibly the military, university students represent the decisive nuclei of both support for and opposition to existing political arrangements. That so many are disgusted, disillusioned, and disenchanted to the point of calculated depoliticization says much about the "politics of despair" characterizing contemporary Moroccan youth.

The confluence of political disillusionment and economic decay is felt most acutely among Morocco's current generation of educated young people—those born in the 1960s—who are characterized by less rigorous academic training, greater exposure to Arabic, with a concurrent decline in bilingual fluency, vulnerability to Islamic appeals, increased support for radical political views, and a turning away from Western values and norms (see Zartman 1973; Waterbury 1970; Tessler 1982; Ashford 1973; and Hermassi 1972).

Although other less-educated groups in society share this sense of hopelessness, they do not necessarily direct their frustrations and bitterness at the political system in general or at the monarchy in particular. Indeed, for the overwhelming majority of ordinary Moroccan men and women, the political "system" is an abstract concept that matters very little in their daily lives. The only national-level political institution that animates their interest is the monarchy, and toward it they are generally supportive.

The following is a composite picture of Moroccans' reactions to politics, processes, and personalities: general public support from the country's traditional and modern elite including its critical military component; depoliticization by the majority of rural and urban bourgeoisie; cynicism and hostility by most educated youth of the Right and Left without, however, their involvement in either "positive" system challenges—participation in and through organized political parties—or "negative" system challenges—their engaging in overt antistate acts of violence and upheaval; political amorphousness among the potentially socially explosive urban underclass and slum dwellers; and massive political apathy and indifference among the majority of ordinary tradition-bound denizens of medium-sized cities and villages, who, nonetheless, give strong support to the monarchy as the embodiment of the national state and the king as "commander of the faithful."

AFFECTIVE DIMENSION

The affective orientation of most Moroccans toward polity, processes, outputs, and leaders is fairly consistent with the cognitive and evaluative dimensions of political culture already discussed. Emotionally, virtually all Moroccans identify with the Muslim consensus; there is a strong sense of personal association with the symbols and historic purpose of the Moroccan nation. While various groups may feel differently about the political system and its actors, all are united in their feelings about the integrity and legitimacy of the Moroccan homeland. This sentiment is evident at all levels of society and expressed in varied circumstances.

As already noted, all Moroccans are especially proud of their country's athletic accomplishments, whether at the 1984 Olympic Games or the 1986 World Cup football (soccer) championship, where Morocco advanced further than any other African country in the history of that prestigious sporting event. The same kind of emotional intensity is evident on the question of the Western Sahara, on which there is virtually universal support for the king's policy of "reintegrating" part of the homeland into Morocco proper. One study of Moroccan junior high school students, for example, confirmed this sense of pride in country, national symbols, and accomplishments, as measured in feelings toward national anthem, flag, and king (Suleiman 1985). The picture emerges of strong affective ties to homeland, *patrie*, or *watan*, a sentiment that appears among the young, extends through adolescence, wanes somewhat during early adulthood (especially at the university level), but then reemerges with even more vigor and intensity in middle age.

Beyond these common national-level affective ties, however, divisions along the other cultural dimensions reflect social group differences. Thus, "toward the present elite, young educated Moroccans display feelings of hostility, contempt, and indifference, but almost never admiration. They are exponents of a sort of glib radicalism, more remarkable for its cynicism than its idealism" (Waterbury 1970, 309). This latter trait is less the case for fundamentalist students whose commitment to puritanical beliefs appears sincere. Clearly the manipulation of the contemporary jargon of Third World socialism has discredited many of the leftists in the eyes of Muslim fundamentalists, among others.

For ordinary Moroccans, affective ties are focused on the primordial and local, rarely extending beyond the village level except, of course, as they apply to the king. Nonetheless, Morocco remains an integrated society. Despite the social pluralism and diversity already discussed, there is no group of any consequence that looks outside the country for political identity or attachment. Berber tribes in Morocco are distinct from and totally independent of Berber groups in Algeria, for example. There is no politically significant nationalist-oriented Berberist movement within the country or transnational sentiment linking Berbers across Morocco and Algeria. The same is true for other distinct groups in the society, whether Jewish, Sahrawi, or those Muslims living within the Spanish enclaves of Melilla and Ceuta. The Sahrawi tribesmen under Moroccan administrative and political control seem loyal and attached to the throne, if not the Moroccan nation. There is to date, for example, no evidence of overt or clandestine opposition to Moroccan rule in the Western Sahara, although not all Sahrawis, who are by tradition and history a very independent-minded people, necessarily identify unswervingly with the entirety of Moroccan political institutions and processes (on the Western Sahara, see Damis 1983; Hodges 1983; and Barbier 1982).

Relatively few Moroccan Jews have remained in the country since their situation became precarious with the founding of the state of Israel. Those that remain exhibit a sense of loyalty to the throne and patriotism for Morocco. As one survey of Moroccan Jews revealed, "The political culture of Moroccan Jewry is characterized by low political involvement, a belief that politics is dominated by powerful individuals and, accordingly, a high degree of respect for authority, and the view that Jewish interests are reasonably well served by this arrangement" (Tessler and Hawkins 1980, 81). Like their Muslim counterparts, Moroccan Jews consider themselves politically powerless and marginal. Both groups reveal a general orientation that regards the government as authoritarian but essentially benevolent.

This sense of marginality is particularly acute with regard to the standing and the status of the king, to whom Jews look for protection and leadership. Anything that endangers King Hassan or his standing among Arabs is perceived as a threat and makes Jews anxious. This was particularly the case when the Israeli prime minister, Shimon Peres, came to visit Hassan in Ifrane, Morocco, in July 1986. Over the years the Jews' intense sense of dependence on the king has bred an insecurity that is palpable. For the elite among them there has always been a strong sense of Moroccan identification. David Amar, for example, the president of the Council of Moroccan Jewish Communities, has indicated: "The Jewish community has traditionally enjoyed a degree of religious freedom in Morocco unknown anywhere else in the Arab world. . . . I am a loyal Moroccan. I love my country and my sovereign" (Miller 1986). Despite the fact that Amar and others like him strongly support Israel, this has neither caused him or his counterparts problems with the Moroccan authorities nor made it difficult for such Jews to remain loyal citizens of the country.

In the coastal Spanish presidios, or enclaves, of Ceuta and Melilla, as along Morocco's northeastern region between the Rif Mountains and the Mediterranean Sea, Berber tribesmen have long exhibited a strong independent streak. A region that historically existed beyond Makhzen influence and control, the Rif suffered considerable social and economic hardship during the years of Spanish colonial rule (1912–1956). Conditions did not improve considerably in the postindependence period; the Northeast as a whole, and particularly the mountain areas, remains relatively disadvantaged and underdeveloped (Seddon 1984). One consequence has been that in this most economically depressed of regions a number of revolts and uprisings have taken place, as in 1958, 1959, and, most recently, in January 1984, due in great part to actual and perceived conditions of inequality, unemployment, and poverty.

Residents in the area have long resented what they have seen as discrimination, maladministration, and neglect from the central authorities (Seddon 1984). For its part, the monarchy has been suspicious of the region's loyalty to the crown, given the earlier republicanism of the northern mountain zones under the rebel Abd el Krim during the 1920s (Seddon 1984). Royalist sympathies probably are weakest there and the potential for social unrest, the greatest in the kingdom.

There have also been historic ties between this northern area of the country and western Algeria. Yet there is no concrete evidence of any irredentist sentiment linking the al-Hoceima and Nador regions, for example, with Algeria that in any way compromises the Riffians' commitment to the territorial integrity and national unity of Morocco.

Muslims living in the presidios seem ambivalent about the prospects of losing the privileges of Spanish legal administration should Ceuta and Melilla be returned to Morocco sometime in the future. (Morocco's official position is that it will not demand the reintegration of these territories until the question of Gibraltar has been resolved.) Yet when Spain does depart, it seems unlikely that those residents would do anything but either accept their new Moroccan status or emigrate to Spain. In sum, although the northeastern coastal region of Morocco has had a long history of independent-mindedness and political recalcitrance, including only tepid affective ties to the throne, the principal grievances against the regime are social and economic in origin and expression and not cultural, ethnic, or tribal.

In conclusion, Moroccan political culture is ambivalent and bifurcated, with incumbent and incipient elites, educated youth, and other politically cognitive segments of the Moroccan population supportive of the Muslim consensus but cynical about the way political power and authority are being used by the monarchy in the name of that consensus. For the overwhelming majority of the apathetic nonelite, however, the monarchy *is* the Muslim consensus—the only national-level institution with which they can identify in a symbolic and affective way.

In either case, the apparent cultural gap between elite and mass political attitudes may not be so severe as assumed, particularly when one refers to some of the key attitudinal indicators often associated with political discontent and opposition. One must be cautious, for example, in interpreting "cynicism," "mistrust," and "alienation" in the Moroccan context. Throughout its long history Moroccans have exhibited these traits in one form or another vis-à-vis those in authority, especially power distantly removed from local concerns. That such traits exist today does not so much indicate hostility to the monarchy per se as it shows the continuation of doubts, suspicions, and insecurity regarding any political power with which one is not personally, familially, or tribally associated. Yes, there is political cynicism in Morocco, but no, it is not caused exclusively by royal corruption or insensitivity. Such sentiment is of historic origin, is rooted in culture and tradition, will take a long time to be significantly modified, and is independent of what kind of regime is in national power—monarchical, modernist (of the radical or republican variety), militarist, or messianic.

Chapter Four

Subcultures

Throughout the centuries, Moroccan social and cultural life has been characterized by divisions and differences, especially ones based on language and ethnicity (Arab-Berber), religion (Muslim-Jew), religious ritual and practice (maraboutic-scripturalist), political authority and organization (*makhzan-siba*), socioeconomic class (Fassi-Soussi), and social organization (rural-urban). While such divisions still exist at the local and personal levels, they have lost much of their significance for national-level politics. This is as true, for example, for the rural-urban split as it is for the ethnolinguistic differences separating Arabs and Berbers. Independent observers (see Gellner and Micaud 1972) agree virtually unanimously that Berber identity does not constitute the basis for a separatist or nationalist political movement. Even the so-called Berberist political party, the Mouvement Populaire (MP), is a mainstream progovernment organization protecting the interests of its rural bourgeoisie clientele.

The Berbers are the indigenous people of North Africa. Their origin is uncertain, but the name probably comes from the Greek, denoting a people not conversant with either Latin or Greek and having alien manners and customs. The Berbers themselves do not use this name. Most commonly they identify themselves by birthplace or tribe. About 40 percent of Morocco's nearly 25 million people are considered linguistically and ethnically Berber. In general, the Berbers tend to be poor, rural, and less educated than the Arabs. The various tribes are not united in any political or special sense. In the past, Berbers have revolted against urban Arab authority, and the French tried to manipulate the Berber tribes against the incipient Moroccan nationalist movement of the 1940s and 1950s.

Some Berber intellectuals complain about discrimination against Berbers in general. They are not allowed to use their language in schools, for example. The failed military coups in 1971 and 1972 against King Hassan were led by Berber officers. These included General Mohamed Oufkir, who had been the leading member of the armed forces and was close to the king. In fact, with the exception of four or five men, almost all Moroccan officers are Berber. Berber officers are found among the opposition and the loyalists. Today the army's Berber officers are considered loyal and reliable. Berber field officers have been granted increased autonomy in combatting the POLISARIO (Popular Front for the Liberation of Saguiat el Hamra and Rio de Oro) in the Western Sahara.

The Berbers of Morocco may take some inspiration from Berbers in Algeria, who have demonstrated in support of various issues on education, culture, and employment. Yet, despite the coup attempts of more than a decade ago, the Berbers continue to look to the king as protector against militant Arabs. Should a strong Arab-Islamic movement emerge in Morocco with support from Hassan, the Berbers and the military would react strongly to counter it.

If Berberism was a recognizable yet declining subcultural cleavage of the past, class conflicts and socioeconomic inequalities will most likely be sources of division for the future. If not attended to in bold and comprehensive fashion, Morocco's social and economic cleavages will deepen and widen to the point of creating serious political unrest capable of overthrowing the regime. In both relative and absolute terms, the gap between rich and poor, urban and rural, educated and illiterate, continues to grow dangerously.

Yet this remains a problem for the intermediate future. For the 1990s, the most serious threat to Moroccan cultural and political integrity comes from Muslim fundamentalist groups. Although the latter feed on the misery, poverty, and economic backwardness of society's underclass, these are not necessarily the causes for the rise of populist Islam; Sociopsychological and cultural factors are of equal, if not greater, importance in explaining Islam's revival in a new and more militant form. In Morocco today, messianic Islam constitutes the most serious vertically structured subcultural cleavage challenging society's dominant culture and competing subcultures.

VERTICALLY STRUCTURED SUBCULTURES

Messianic Islam (alternative labels include: *intégrisme*, Islamism, militant or radical Islam, fundamentalism, populist Islam, and Islamic revivalism) has emerged in Morocco as elsewhere in the Arab-Islamic world in response to a complex and interactive set of economic, political, sociopsychological, and cultural dislocations and discontinuities, of both domestic and external origin, which have buffeted the nation in recent years. Pervasive economic and social problems have created a widespread sense of disillusionment, disaffection, and despair among many dislocated groups in the population. Both real and perceived conditions of social inequality, limited economic opportunity, a calcified political system, and cultural degeneration have led many semieducated men and women living on the economic periphery of large cities to turn to the basis of cultural tradition and identity for salvation—Islam. Overurbanization, rural migration, the loss of communal identity, the comings and goings of migrant workers to Europe—all these factors have created a mass of alienated and marginalized individuals who are open to Muslim appeals for salvation, redemption, and hope (see Etienne and Tozy 1979).

Although current socioeconomic and political problems have created the context for mass discontent, it is the perceived assault on cultural identity, symbols, and practices that has galvanized individuals toward messianic movements and radical action. Throughout history and in all societies there have been extremist responses, including acts of fanaticism and terror, to conditions of social turmoil and unrest.

Fanaticism, whether of an Islamic or other variety, breeds on social upheavals, which leave people feeling dislocated as though they and their world were falling apart. As many of Morocco's marginalized urban malcontents are discovering, the loss of traditions that give meaning to life leaves people prey to extreme ideologies. Clinging to some absolute truth brings a sense of stability and relief. The hallmark of the fanatic's ideology is an apocalyptic vision that divides the world into good and evil. This view, joined with a strong sense of hopelessness, leads those who take the next step to join and participate in fundamentalist movements. This next step takes place when the sense of hopelessness turns into burning rage. This stage has not yet been reached in Morocco.

Individuals with that burning rage have neither the expectation nor the hope of being anything other than powerless for the rest of their lives. Many perceive themselves as rootless and victimized. Fundamentalists describe a current or imminent conflict between the forces of good (Islam) and evil (non-Islam), in which the forces of evil will prevail at first but will ultimately be defeated by the forces of good. The victory will mark the end of the present era, and the initiation of a new era of peace, harmony, and general exaltation. Although a bleak and angry outlook is typical of those who grow up in circumstances of oppression, many more people share such feelings than ever join an extremist or militant organization. Yet for those who do—and in Morocco they still remain a politically insignificant minority—messianic Islam constitutes the most compelling and persuasive idiom for political mobilization.

Islamism differs from its traditional antecedents in several important ways. Unlike "traditional" religious belief, which finds expression through individual devoutness and communal identity, populist Islam seeks to translate religious sentiment into direct sociopolitical action. Additionally, whereas official or reformist Islam remains conservative, "sanctioning and making sacred the world as it is" (Lapidus 1983, 64), radical Islam is bent on the total transformation of the world, according to some fixed ideal. Finally, whereas the established religious order preaches piety in order to achieve salvation in the afterlife, populist Islam insists on redemption and fulfillment in the present. In sum, militant religious movements "are powerful psychological and political forces precisely because they mobilize the religious yearning for salvation and project it into modern politics. The revival embodies a totalistic and utopian dream of a perfected human condition—not only in private morals but in political life, not in the next world but in this one" (Lapidus 1983, 64).

In the Moroccan context, discontent with existing structures of social inequality and a generalized belief that government is only interested in increasing the wealth of incumbent elites (see Eickelman 1985; Etienne and Tozy 1979) are articulated in deeply moral terms intended to link failures of socioeconomic development with the immoral and "un-Islamic" practices of secular-minded political leaders. In the newspaper of the major revivalist movement in the country, for example, one finds such condemnations as: "Morocco has become [the Arab] brothel since the destruction of Beirut"; "Sexual depravity has made of Morocco the nest of international prostitution"; "It is in our 'democratic' system that one finds the origins of all our troubles"; and "A quarter of a century of independence has passed and we are now more tied to the infidel than ever before" (Etienne and Tozy 1979, 253).

From its very onset, militant Islam has been devoted to reforming individual and collective behavior, which it sees as indissolubly interrelated. In this sense Islamism expresses the deeply rooted Muslim assumption about the relation of religion and politics that has been part of the faith since its inception. These assumptions differ profoundly from the understanding Americans have of "church-state" relations. As Lapidus has indicated:

> For Muslims all economic and political problems are at bottom moral problems. . . . The basis of a good and powerful Muslim society is people with belief in Islam, virtuous impulses, and commitment to religious law. A good society stems ultimately from the goodness of men. Americans, on the contrary, tend to think that a well-run economic and political society is regulated by the legitimate competition of interests. . . . Americans believe that the free . . . competition of interest generates a healthy and powerful society. Traditional Muslim thought sees the competition of interests as immoral and government institutions to regulate and channel such competition as worse than useless. For Muslims a healthy, powerful, and just society stems from the good behavior of individuals,

and the route to a just and powerful society is through the reform of the hearts and minds of men—through the practice of, and belief in, and commitment to Islam (1980, 99).

There have always existed separate groups, movements, and organizations concerned with defending the faith against corrupting or alien influences. Such "associations for the defense of Islam" continue to operate in Morocco today, often with the approval and support of government authorities, who condone such associations as long as they limit their preachings to religious affairs in the mosques. Those promoting fundamentalist beliefs, however, have totally bypassed these groupings to form their own associations. In one study of such associations in Casablanca, for example, it was found that they differed in three important ways from their government-approved counterparts: First, meetings are held discreetly if not secretly at the homes of association members where "experts" preach on Islamic subjects; second, their purpose is to replace completely those Islamic defense associations, which are considered ineffective and hopelessly compromised; and finally, these militant associations have more direct and constant contact with the Arabo-Muslim world than they have with Morocco's politico-religious hierarchy (see Etienne and Tozy 1979, 248).

This religious "counterculture" does not constitute a single group or association, however. There are an estimated twenty to forty such groups in existence countrywide; only a handful are of any real significance. Their methods are to conduct regular meetings not only in private homes but also in universities, high schools, and mosques, bringing together believers and nonbelievers, political activists as well as those indifferent to politics, for the purpose of discussing religious issues. Their initial aim is to create a Muslim public opinion, which, according to activist leaders, does not currently exist. Only later, and after proper ideological inculcation, do *intégristes* envision the creation of a formal organization. To date, they have been quite successful in utilizing popular sports clubs and athletic groups as the forum for religious instruction and mobilization. In the Casablanca study, for example, karate clubs were one particular avenue for politico-religious socialization, creating both spiritually prepared as well as physically conditioned recruits (Etienne and Tozy 1979, 248).

There are three principal and competing fundamentalist associations. The Association of Islamic Youth is headed by a veteran Muslim militant (Abdelkrim Mottei) who was a former school inspector. He was condemned to death three times and currently shuttles between Europe and certain Arab capitals promoting his radical views. He preaches the need for "armed struggle" and the overthrow of the Moroccan monarchy. It is alleged that he has ties to Algeria's secret service.

The Movement of Moudjahidines (fighters in the cause of Islam) is led by Mottei's former right-hand man, Abdelaziz Enaamani. He was previously a liberal arts student in Rabat and was twice condemned to death by Moroccan authorities. He is said to be close to the Iranian clerical elite. He was living in exile in France until September 25, 1985, when he supposedly "disappeared." According to his associates, he was "abducted," a victim of an in-house settling of scores.

The most publicized group, which has no formal organization but is best known for its magazine, Al Jamaa (The community), is headed by Abdessalem Yassin. Yassin, a political prisoner from 1974 to 1977 and the most prominent leader of Morocco's nonofficial Islamic movement, claims to be a purer Muslim than King Hassan. He is a strong supporter of Khomeini in Iran and has called for a military coup.

After his release from prison in 1978, Yassin founded Al Jamaa, which criticizes the government partly on religious grounds. Yassin is estimated to have nearly 4,000 loyal followers, some of whom may have been associated with the Association of Islamic Youth. (This youth group took responsibility in 1975 for the assassination of Omar Benjelloun, a prominent figure in the Union Socialiste des Forces Populaires [USFP], the country's premier left-wing opposition party.) Yassin predicts a Muslim revival in Morocco because no party or trade union really represents the masses, while the state itself is becoming more and more corrupt. He has been imprisoned since 1983 for alleged antistate activities.

The following characteristics accurately describe the diverse groups espousing Muslim militancy that have proliferated in

Morocco in recent years: They are organizationally diffuse; the mosque is the principal but not exclusive forum for the dissemination of their messages; their membership is predominantly male of village or small-town origin but currently residing in an urban environment and experiencing rapid and disruptive socioeconomic change; all members of the groups are very politically aware and knowledgeable about political developments in the country and out; their recruitment is accomplished mainly through word-of-mouth and person-to-person contact; supporters of these movements do not come from the sons and daughters of the incumbent political elite; none are affiliated with established political organizations or movements, which, in any case, are perceived as ineffective; financial support comes from both within and without Morocco; and finally, these neo-Muslim movements reject both saintly and scripturalist Islam on intellectual, moral, and leadership grounds (see Eickelman 1985).

Those who lead, follow, and support such movements represent a heterogenous group of men and women. In their survey of Muslim militants in Casablanca, for example, Etienne and Tozy found a broad spectrum of social types involved in such activity, including students (high school and university), schoolteachers, craftsmen, shopkeepers, and other elements of the middle class (1979). But the bulk of mass support and sympathy comes from the urban periphery: from those living in lower-class quarters in and bidonvilles of large urban centers such as Casablanca. It is in such milieus that one finds recent rural emigrants who are rootless and alienated in urban society. Both the petite bourgeoisie and the marginalized urban dweller share a common feeling of despair, which socioeconomic hardships have made more acute. For most of these people the invocation of the successful anticolonial struggle, pride in achieving political independence, and the reassertion of the native monarchical rule are insufficient to overcome the profound sense of disaffection and despair. Messianic culture is uniquely compelling for such people.

The typical convert to the "cause" is a Muslim who, after abrupt conversion, decides to respect what he believes to be the principles of the faith. This individualistic effort at improving the image he has of himself is accompanied by a similar effort at transforming Morocco into a Muslim state whose function would be to apply these religious beliefs to the whole of society (Etienne and Tozy 1979).

Manifestations of this religiosity are evident throughout contemporary Morocco. It is apparent in such symbolically important acts as personal appearance (men wearing beards) and clothing (women wearing the *hijab*, a habit covering the whole body save the face), in the popularity of religious figures possessing strong or charismatic qualities, the increased purchases of magazines, books, cassettes, and movies on Islamic subjects, increased mosque attendance and individual piety (as measured by those performing the required rituals more faithfully), and greater attention given to popular (read: Islamic) culture as a whole.

As the authors of the Casablanca study discovered, the views of the hard-core militants are revolutionary by Moroccan standards. Their views can be summarized as follows:

- The political class is amoral, incompetent, and without conscience.
- Sooner or later a military man (a *mahdi*) will mobilize the frustrated people against this class.
- Cabinet ministers follow the king blindly—"if he says white, they say white; if he says black, they say black."
- There are only two entities: the state and religion; thus the Alawite's claim of fusing both in the institution of the monarchy is rejected.
- The "commander of the faithful" is like all other believers— if he makes mistakes he must conform to the contract. No mortal has religious authority because God has not relegated that authority to any man.
- Power is through God as exercised by the *umma*. Islam does not recognize hereditary power, thus rejecting Alawite application of primogeniture in effect since 1961.
- *Intégristes* reject the notion that the king has *baraka*, or divine grace.
- And finally, people must listen with their hearts and not their minds (Etienne and Tozy 1979, 258–259).

The Islamic idiom used by the militants is meant to appeal "to both threatened and aspiring classes who use it to articulate the need for political protection, on the one hand, and a restoration of the moral order, on the other. [Such] activism generally represents a minority opposition to the religious mentality, political power, and economic interests of the dominant groups in society and especially of the state elites" (Lapidus 1983, 630).

Despite its revolutionary potential, messianic culture still remains very much a minority orientation. In both the cities and in the countryside the overwhelming majority of Moroccans reject neo-Muslim solutions to problems of socioeconomic and political change. Surveys of university students, for example, show continued commitment to a secular-sectarian balance of increased religiosity in personal and collective behavior (see Tozy 1984 and Munson 1986). Tozy's student sample of 400, for example, showed that while the majority remained faithful to Islam as religion and cultural form, only a small percentage (under 5 percent) endorsed a militant concept of Islam as a political ideology (see Tozy 1984 and Munson 1986, 273). Support for this latter sentiment was even weaker in the countryside. Among rural folk in particular, the activism of populist Islam still does not seriously challenge the primacy of religious legitimacy embodied in king and throne. This is not to underestimate the social and political significance of revivalist Islam: Numbers per se are not determinative of potential system change. Numbers are important, however, in terms of cultural change, and in this regard the overwhelming majority of Moroccans— "the silent majority"—identify with the Muslim consensus, that is, the synthesis of saintly and scripturalist belief embodied in the royal institution.

The monarchy itself is not remaining impassive in the face of these Islamic challenges. Following the January 1984 nationwide riots, for example, the government came down hard on fundamentalists, arresting many leaders, closing down offices, and confiscating journals and other publications. Given the threatening posture of militant Islam in neighboring Algeria and Tunisia and the capacity for mischief making at home, it seems unlikely that the king, especially since the 1984 riots, will allow fundamentalists the kind of leeway they enjoyed prior to the Iranian revolution in 1979.

As a security measure, mosques in certain quarters of Casablanca have been closed during nonpraying hours so as to better monitor their use. There are of course negative implications for the regime in any such endeavor; indeed, "any form of intervention in religious activities is a serious matter for a ruler claiming religious legitimacy" (Eickelman 1986, 184). More effective would be the politics of co-optation that the monarch has used over the years as part of his strategy for keeping potential counterelites in line. Hassan can attempt to co-opt leaders of militant Islamic movements as well. Since so much of the population accepts the religious foundations of the monarchy, this process would not be so difficult as in Tunisia and Algeria for example (see Leveau 1985 and Eickelman 1986, 185).

This is not to imply that Islamism can be treated like any other oppositional group or tendency. If there is one feature about militant Islam that distinctly separates it from its secular and mainstream religious competitors, it is its total indifference to material or status blandishments, which the throne could possibly offer in return for compliance and subordination. Indeed, the fact remains "that some vaguely militant preachers sympathetic to the malleable notions of an Islamic state and society are expressing widespread grievances in a religious idiom that is highly appealing to the great majority of Moroccan Muslims" (Munson 1986, 284).

HORIZONTALLY STRUCTURED SUBCULTURES

The lines separating cooperative, competitive, and conflictual interactions among Morocco's monarchical, modernist, militarist, and messianic orientations are extremely fine. Messianic culture has demonstrated clear evidence of transforming itself into a full-blown counterculture involving opposition to the regime's cultural, social, economic, as well as political policies. Although its current political impact is still minor, the fact that it appeals directly to Morocco's masses makes it potentially the most influential of countercultural trends. The modernist and militarist perspectives appeal to a much narrower segment of society— its educated and elite stratum.

Modernist political culture applies to the liberal wing of Morocco's sociopolitical elites as well as to the more radical *gauchistes*, who espouse neo-Marxist formulas. Members of both groups have at one time or another cooperated with the monarchy in order to advance more effectively their narrow clientelist interests. More often, however, they have been competing with the throne in order to curry favor with their real and potential followers. In recent years left-wing extremists have turned against the king completely, even going as far as to ally themselves politically with the POLISARIO, the guerrilla organization fighting Morocco for control of the Western Sahara. In each instance, modernist political culture represents but a limited grouping in society—the university-educated liberal arts graduates of middle-class and upper-middle-class background who live in urban areas.

In the past, the thinking and political orientation of Mehdi Ben Barka would have come closest to representing the radical Left. Although Ben Barka embodied leftist and radical political trends, as reflected in his characteristically Marxist vocabulary and occasionally radical methods, at heart he was no dogmatist or doctrinaire leftist, for he could be remarkably pragmatic about attaining already defined objectives. Ben Barka's split with the Istiqlal—the leading bourgeois party of nationalist independence—in 1959 and the creation of the National Union of Popular Forces (UNFP) represented a high mark for secular radical politics in Morocco. With his disappearance and assassination in France in 1965, however, the Left effectively lost its most charismatic and popular leader. The UNFP was unable to maintain its radical credentials and was itself superseded in 1974 by a left-wing offshoot of the party, the USFP (Socialist Union of Popular Forces). It, along with Morocco's officially recognized Communist party (Parti du Progrès et du Socialisme, PPS), today constitute mainstream radicalism (read: liberalism).

For all practical purposes, the extreme, neo-Marxist Left has gone underground or overseas, especially to France where it calls for the overthrow of the monarchy and the establishment of a socialist republic. Both liberalism and *gauchisme* have been in retreat in recent years, as monarchical power and messianic appeals have vied for the hearts and minds of Moroccans. Nonetheless, liberal politicians and political parties continue to play by the rules of the game, participating, for example, in the 1984 legislative elections, where they performed relatively well. The same cannot be said of the *gauchistes*. They have been on the defensive since the middle 1970s, both on university campuses and among radical unions and workers.

Whereas the liberal subculture is divided between liberals and *gauchistes*, and both are at the mercy of the king's carrot-and-stick policies (carrot for the liberals, stick for the *gauchistes*), the militarist subculture stands out as the great unknown. As already noted, the officer class of the FAR, the Royal Armed Forces, is made up overwhelmingly of Berbers from the countryside. Yet their ethnolinguistic origin is less important than their extremely conservative and nationalistic political views, which stress the need for discipline, honesty, and sacrifice at the expense of democracy, liberty, and justice.

The army's relations with the monarchy have been unpredictable. As crown prince, Hassan was given the task of modernizing the military while ensuring its loyalty to the throne. It appeared as if he had performed well in those capacities, for the army was supportive of the young king at his ascendancy to the throne in 1961. Yet, within two years, a military conspiracy was discovered and had to be put down. The military was also given the "dirty" task of assassinating Ben Barka, with General Mohamed Oufkir, then Moroccan minister of the interior, and Colonel Ahmed Dlimi, then chief of the Sûreté Nationale, directly implicated by France in the plot. It was no accident, given their prior dissatisfaction with the way the king and ruling elites abused political power, that Oufkir in 1971 and 1972 and Dlimi in 1983 were behind real and alleged plots against the king.

Although it appears today that the Moroccan military is loyal to the throne, in great measure due to the many real and symbolic advantages the army has gained from its battlefield successes in the Western Sahara, there is no guarantee that this loyalty will endure. The military mind-set and political culture remain at odds with the other cultural orientations. Yet, unlike the monarchy, liberal politicians, left-wing radicals, or Muslim militants, the military has the capacity to act on its beliefs, especially under conditions of socioeconomic turmoil, political disarray, or military defeat in the Sahara war.

Waterbury's assessment of Morocco's army officers, made in 1970, is still applicable nearly two decades later: "The guardians of the state's coercive power, they are of incalculable political significance simply because they are there, semi-unknown, in the back of all civilian minds, a sort of lurking threat . . . forming an inescapable backdrop against which all political decisions are made" (1970, 84).

INSTITUTIONAL SUBCULTURES

Morocco's institutional subcultures that merit special attention are the business community, labor unions, the military, political parties, and student groups. Each will be discussed in turn.

Much of the domestic and foreign trade is controlled by urban families descended from Arabs who were expelled from Spain in the fifteenth and sixteenth centuries. Many settled in Fez, the center of business power until the early part of the twentieth century. Casablanca is now the country's primary commercial center. It is one of Africa's busiest cities and Morocco's most populous city.

Members of the Fez economic elite dominate the textile industry and trade, although they have also moved into other areas. Because of their better education and skills, they have moved into positions of power within the government and have favored policies that protected their business interests.

The Fez families are rivaled in economic power by the Berber Soussi, or persons from the Sous River valley, who have tended to dominate the food retailing and wholesaling business. Many retailers in the cities are descendants of members of the few Soussi tribes that migrated to the urban areas during the nineteenth century and started small grocery businesses. The initial success of the first ventures brought many other Soussi families north, and retailing became an occupation for them. After World War II, the more successful Soussi merchants became wholesalers or moved into other kinds of businesses. Despite economic rivalries between the Arab Fez and the Berber Soussi groups, they often pool their resources to make joint investments in new endeavors.

Both groups have amassed great wealth and would be targets of any populist uprising of the Left or Right. They have close ties with both the government and foreign businesses. One group or the other is usually the partner in the joint equity ventures required of certain business investments. The Fez and Soussi business families have also profited most from the nationalization of French-owned lands.

These two groups are often accused of flaunting their wealth and are criticized for refusing to encourage reforms with a new pattern of distribution of benefits, which would help undermine any revolutionary movement. The Islamic leaders regard them as sinners, because Morocco imports great quantities of alcoholic beverages, some of it for these economic elites. To many nationalists and fundamentalists, these wealthy and influential families symbolize the corruption and inequities in Morocco.

The Moroccan trade union movement developed as a result of industrialization during the French Protectorate (1912–1956), although a rudimentary form of trade unionism has existed for centuries in the various handicraft occupations of such cities as Fez. The first Moroccan trade union was organized in Casablanca as an affiliate of the French Confédération Générale du Travail (CGT) and had a membership primarily made up of port workers.

In 1955, Tayyib Bouazza and Mahjoub Ben Seddiq, who had served jail sentences for organizing a general strike, founded the Union Marocaine du Travail (UMT). The UMT worked closely with the Istiqlal party on behalf of independence. When a political split occurred among the Istiqlal leaders, the UMT aligned itself organizationally with the National Union of Popular Forces (UNFP). In 1960, the Istiqlal set up a rival trade union, the General Union of Moroccan Workers (UGTM). However, the UGTM has never attracted membership in numbers comparable to those of the UMT.

The UMT is not really independent of the elite establishment. Like other elements of the political Left, it opposes the government on policy but accepts the rules of the system. The UMT leaders are regularly consulted by the king on important policy issues and many also hold government positions, leading younger union militants to question the validity of such constructive opposition. The UMT has kept its position among the rank and file by emphasizing jobs and economic benefits rather than politics. The UMT's reluctance to engage in radical activities is reinforced by the fact that the government provides the organization with all of its offices and pays for all its utilities. Still headed by Ben Seddiq, the UMT claims a membership of over 700,000.

The General Union of Moroccan Workers is headed by Abderrazzaq Afilal; it reportedly has 500,000 members. The UGTM is associated with the Istiqlal party, but is even less independent of the rest of the elite than the UMT is. Consequently, the UGTM has never been effective politically.

In 1978 a new socialist-oriented union, the Democratic Workers Confederation (CDT), with links to the Socialist Union of Popular Forces (USFP), was founded in Casablanca. Its radical image has helped to expand its membership in such important fields as education, transportation, and the phosphate industry.

The union was involved in the labor unrest in 1978 and 1979 in Casablanca. The labor agitation of that period signaled general discontent with the regime and also raised the possibility of increased trade union activism, which had not been seen for a decade. In the sporadic strikes of 1978 and 1979 the CDT rapidly overtook the UMT in prominence and militancy.

The union's most recent protest occurred in June 1981, when it held to its general strike call to protest the government's reduction in food subsidies. (There was no evidence of trade union involvement in the bloody "bread riots" of January 1984). The CDT's attempt to organize public demonstrations degenerated in Casablanca into riots in which roaming mobs attacked symbols of public authority and numerous businesses. The violence caused many deaths; estimates range from the government's figure of 66 to the USFP's figure of 635. One-third of the executive committee of the CDT, the 9 members of the union's National Bureau, and nearly 100 local leaders of the USFP were arrested. Although the subsequent release of the USFP leaders has soothed government and labor relations, the stature of the CDT as a radical force of the Left, capable and willing to engage authorities, is high among many of the regime's opposition groups.

Despite the UMT's historic role and the CDT's occasional success in opposing the regime, the political and economic climate in Morocco remains hostile to the development of a vigorous and independent labor movement. Three particular factors inhibit such development. First, the high level of unemployment makes the unions insecure and vulnerable to sudden, unplanned changes in membership, recruitment, financial support, and organizational solidarity. Second, the unions are subject to harsh pressure and blandishments from the government. Moreover, very serious differences exist between trade union interests and those of the politicians. Finally, the constant factor of monarchical manipulation accentuates divisions instead of fostering unity in the labor movement, just as it has with the opposition political parties.

Until 1971, the Royal Armed Forces, or more specifically, senior military officers, were the source of the monarchy's staunchest support. Many of the senior officers had held commissions in the French or Spanish military and had even participated in operations against the independence movement. Despite this fact, or because of it, Mohamed V allowed them to return to Morocco to form the nucleus of the FAR. The monarch's policy of constantly shifting military commands prevented the officers from developing significant personal constituencies, thus reinforcing their loyalty to the throne.

When Hassan became crown prince in 1957, he was appointed chief of staff of the FAR. He enlarged the armed forces and ensured that their material requirements were met. Furthermore, he steadily integrated the senior officers into the royal patronage system, a task made easier because, as chief of staff, he decided promotions. After becoming king in 1961, Hassan divided Morocco into military regions, each directed by a trusted officer.

The FAR has historically been staffed by Berbers because, at independence, men from the Army of Liberation and Moroccans in the French and Spanish armies combined to form the armed forces of Morocco. The Army of Liberation was dominated by Berber soldiers, who subsequently entered the rank and file of the FAR. The officer corps of the new army was composed principally of men educated at Azrou and Meknes who had served with the French forces. These men also tended to be sons of wealthy and prominent rural families.

The rural and Berber character of the army elite served not only to maintain order for the king but also to act as a political counterweight to the leftist Istiqlal party and the urban establishment. Army officers, for their part, were generally eager to participate in this alliance, believing in an apolitical military loyal to the state. They also believed that strong ties to the palace were the best way to keep the rural and Berber world from being dominated by the urban Arab elite, although they were not advocates of Berber nationalism. Finally, they recognized that the army provided an important avenue for personal mobility and for access to resources, enabling them to participate in the same national spoils system as other elite groups. With the attempted coups d'état of 1971 and 1972, however, the alliance between the military and the king was badly shaken.

The senior army officers who led the coups appear to have been sincerely frustrated by corruption and the general political drift. Probably many were worried about their own status as well. The failed coups shook the political leadership and dealt a severe blow to the king's confidence in his political alliances, for King Hassan felt he knew, individually and collectively, the high-ranking officers of his army. The events in 1971 and 1972 showed that the military's traditions of loyalty and neutrality could not be counted on to override personal and political discontent. The army officers were clearly seeking to establish a military republic that would once and for all eliminate the corruption in the royal regime. In the years since those events the king has liquidated the disloyal officers and created a more professionally oriented army. Its missions in the Golan Heights in 1973, in Shaba province in Zaire, and currently in the Western Sahara have associated the military prominently with popular and prestigious national causes. This has rebuilt the status of senior army officers, tied them more firmly to Hassan, and given the king an opportunity to provide them with substantial material benefits. The army's budget doubled between 1974 and 1978.

It appeared that by the early 1980s the army had once again become staunchly loyal to the king and his military policies, especially his strong nationalist stand on the annexed territories in the Western Sahara. Continued successes on the battlefield, including the progressive construction of half a dozen desert "walls," which virtually enclose the whole of the disputed territory, seemed destined to keep the army loyal into the indefinite future.

Yet, in January 1983, a military plot was discovered and senior officers were arrested. Shortly thereafter, General Ahmed Dlimi, King Hassan's longtime military adviser and the most important army officer in the country, died in an automobile "accident." Dlimi had directed the successful Saharan campaign and was the architect of Operation Ouhoud, one of FAR's most effective battlefield engagements. Although the full details of Dlimi's suspicious death have never been disclosed, it is assumed that persons loyal to Hassan carried out the killing in advance of a planned military coup.

Although King Hassan has apparently been able to reassert control over the armed forces, the prospect that they will remain indifferent to the profound social dislocations that are occurring in the society can never be a certain one. To this scenario must be added the changing social background and educational levels of new army recruits and younger officers, who are less committed to patrimonial attachments and the power of local and national patrons, including the king. The younger military officers seem more inclined to question the existing political order than do older officers. The younger officers are also more likely to be of urban and Arab origin than the generation that preceded them in the military. Their urban families have actively worked to launch these men into military careeers. The more stringent educational requirements for admission to the military academy have also tended to favor middle-class men from the Arab coastal cities. Thus, there are beginning to appear newly politicized army officers who may become restless should they conclude that their personal advancement is being retarded by conservative old officers. In this situation, personal and political grievances might converge, undermining loyalty to the king and possibly even providing a stimulus to political action. Adding further to the political significance of the military, which grew to over 200,000 men in the wake of the war in the Sahara, is the dramatic increase in its functional weight.

Political party activities in Morocco rarely involve more than a minority of the population, largely because only 40 percent of the population is literate and apathy is widespread among the masses. A tendency to form factions is reflected in the range of political parties, many of which suffer from internal disunity, personal rivalries, and poorly articulated programs. Voting across a party line is quite common.

The leaders of most of the political parties have worked with King Hassan, either as members of the prime minister's cabinet or as members of the National Defense Council. (The defense council was founded in 1979 to advise the king on matters concerning the Sahara war and relations with Algeria.) The party leaders are often middle-class professionals. It is widely believed that they are manipulated on most issues by the king. Even if they are not, it is not clear how large or loyal their constituencies are. In any case, most tend to be from urban rather than rural constituencies. Inasmuch as the monarchy is unwilling to see political parties become either too strong and independent or so weak that they might disappear, the distinction between "parties of support" and "parties of opposition" is not a very meaningful one (Waterbury 1970, 247).

Though none of Morocco's political parties is autonomous, there are important differences among them with respect to both structure and influence. The Rassemblement National des Indépendants (RNI), which held an absolute majority in the assembly elected in 1977, is more of an informal electoral front than an institutionalized political party. It is dominated by rural notables and men from leading urban families who are longtime associates of the king, and its platform is based principally on "unconditional loyalty" to Hassan. The RNI split in 1981, with rural elements breaking away to form a separate faction, the Parti National Démocratique (PND). The RNI and PND fared less well in the 1984 election (RNI = 64; PND = 24) (see Sehimi 1985).

The biggest winner in 1984 was the Union Constitutionelle (UC), a new party formed in 1983. The UC is more of a centrist party than either the RNI or the PND, and its cadres, for the most part, are younger than those of the other two. In the 1984 elections it made a special attempt to appeal to youth and presented itself as a movement committed to addressing social and economic problems. Nevertheless, although its leader had been a trade unionist early in his political career, the party was created with strong backing from the king, and, like the RNI and PND, it lacks a grass-roots base and is highly dependent on the palace for legitimacy and support.

The Mouvement Populaire (MP) bears some resemblance to the parties mentioned earlier. It is dominated by conservative rural notables tied to the palace and does not have an independent platform or ideology. At the same time, as the party of leading Berber families in the north and central mountain regions, it is much older and has a secure electoral base. The party was established in 1957 by men who had led resistance to French colonialism in the rural areas.

Only two parties are institutionalized and have an appeal that does not depend on an ability to extract favors from the palace. These are the Istiqlal (PI) and the Union Socialiste des Forces Populaires (USFP). Formed during the anticolonial struggle against France, the PI is the party of Moroccan nationalism, and under the direction of its founding father and venerable leader, Allal al-Fassi, it was a major force in the years after independence. Al-Fassi died in 1973. The PI did reasonably well in the 1977 balloting, largely because of its historic role, its longtime advocacy of Morocco's claim to the Sahara, and its organizational strength in urban areas. The PI's weaknesses include a lack of appeal in the countryside and a conservative ideology that many Moroccans regard as outdated. These factors contributed to the party's poor showing in 1984.

The USFP traces its origins to a faction (the UNFP) that broke with the Istiqlal in 1959, after charging the latter's leadership with being too conservative. As its name suggests, the USFP is a socialist-oriented party of the Left. Its support comes principally from the trade union movement, from other working-class elements and the urban poor, as well as Morocco's small community of intellectuals. The party's symbolic leader and ideologue was Mehdi Ben Barka, an original founder of the splinter group. As indicated earlier, because of his opposition to the king, Ben Barka was kidnapped by Moroccan security agents in France in 1965 and subsequently killed. The USFP is the principal and most long-standing opponent of the governments formed by the king, although it has occasionally joined the ruling coalition temporarily for tactical reasons. The USFP did poorly in the 1977 elections and was the victim of electoral interference in the local elections of 1983. It did better in the balloting of 1984, however, with its appeal apparently increased by growing social and economic problems.

A number of minor, weakly organized, independent and promonarchy parties round out the political party system. Outside these groupings are several clandestine radical political fringe organizations, including reactionary, religiously oriented groups on the right, and revolutionary Marxist-Leninist-oriented parties on the left, known collectively as Frontists.

University students in Morocco constitute an outspoken element in the country's political life. Relatively small numbers of young people achieve university status; and because a university degree is a virtual prerequisite for elite level positions, the political orientation of students is significant. The National Union of Moroccan Students (UNEM) is the major student organization. Since the 1960s the UNEM has been extensively involved in extralegal and radical activities directed against the regime and its incumbents. Through this or other organizations or as individual-issue interest groups, students have demonstrated over a wide range of educational, political, social, and economic causes, such as Palestinianism, Arab nationalism, revolutionism, anti-imperialism, and antineocolonialism.

In recent years, students have also become increasingly disenchanted with political and social conditions in Morocco, notwithstanding their general support for the regime's policies in the Western Sahara. As job opportunities after graduation continue to diminish, increased student discontent with the existing state of political affairs has led the more radical youths to move even further left.

The students suffer from the same factional and parochial weakness as the political parties. Therefore, UNEM has little ability to influence government policy. Its strikes and demonstrations in the early and middle 1970s failed to intimidate the regime or elicite major gains. Instead, their organization was banned. The UNEM was legalized again in 1978, and it is resuming its activism. For example, it supported the demonstrators in the 1981 and 1984 riots. Its organizational capacity is now limited, however, and most of its leaders do not hold political positions.

The UNEM may eventually be able to exert more political influence than it has thus far. The burgeoning birthrate, the large numbers of young people in the population, the stagnant economy, and the political conservatism among the system's elite make it unlikely that the students can be neutralized indefinitely as a political force. With the passage of time their frustrations are likely to give way to increasingly militant activity.

A small core of leftist militants are already challenging the regime directly and fundamentally. They oppose the war in the Sahara, not only decrying its domestic consequences, but also asserting that the POLISARIO, rather than Hassan, is the legitimate representative of the people of the Western Sahara. Further, they criticize the Moroccan political system, claiming that the democratization process, involving elections, political parties, and parliamentary activity has been a sham. Nor has democratization brought about any meaningful redistribution of wealth and political power. These Frontists have found support mainly among student circles but also among younger and more militant elements within the trade unions and leftist parties. Such militants, who are Marxist-Leninist rather than socialist, sometimes operate from abroad, where they form ties to other opponents of Morocco, such as those from countries aligned with the POLISARIO and senior Moroccan exiles like Mohamed el Basri.

As we have seen, however, most disaffected students in Morocco are turning increasingly to militant Islam rather than to Marxism as the ideological expression of their social discontent. Islamism is beginning to attract students from the lyceés and university campuses. Given the current paralysis of UNEM and the political irrelevance of doctrinaire Marxism as espoused by small groups of students in Morocco and abroad, fundamentalist movements have the greatest potential for transforming themselves from a powerless institutional subculture into a dynamic counterculture.

CULTURE AND FOREIGN POLICY

The Muslim consensus plays a minor if not inconsequential role in the determination and implementation of Moroccan foreign policy. Zartman has made a similar point more boldly and dramatically in trying to explain "the nearly inexplicable"—the absence of Islam in Moroccan foreign policy. "Contrary to current images and expectations, it is probably safe to state as a fact as well as an interpretation that Islam is unnecessary to both the conduct and the context of Moroccan foreign policy, and that it appears only to some lesser extent among its symbols of presentation. . . . Islam figures only secondarily among the referent values that give that policy meaning and legitimacy to its subjects and objects alike" (1983, 97).

Unlike his approach to domestic matters, where development policy is carefully attuned to cultural, religious, and historic considerations, King Hassan's foreign policy is guided by a combination of personal opportunism and a broadly defined national interest. As with all issues related to national-level politics, foreign policy decisions in Morocco are made by the narrow stratum of incumbent political elites that revolves around the monarch. Whereas pluralist tendencies are evident in certain sectors of Moroccan domestic life, no such pluralism exists in the articulation, deliberation, and implementation of foreign policy. Overall, Morocco's foreign policy objectives are to enhance King Hassan's domestic prestige and to protect the status of the political elite; to generate international support for the country's struggle to reintegrate the Western Sahara; to cultivate close economic, technical, and military ties with the West, especially France and United States; and to maintain a symbolic and, increasingly, substantive association with the Afro-Arab, Latin American, and Islamic worlds.

Morocco's continuing strong ties to France are in part a response to geopolitical and economic realities and in part a function of historic conditioning. They also are a reflection of the elite's close affinity with French culture, language, and civilization. These latter characteristics are not shared by the population at large or even by certain portions of the educated classes, a fact that highlights the discontinuity between elite and mass culture despite the regime's formal policy of cultural synthesis. As a result, there is some uncertainty about the extent to which the Moroccan people share in government's strong pro-Western orientation, including its warm and friendly relations with the United States that even the now-defunct Moroccan "union" with the U.S. archenemy, Libya, could not diminish.

France and the United States have rewarded Morocco's moderation in world affairs by becoming the predominant suppliers of military aid—so crucial in its war effort against the POLISARIO—and substantial contributors of economic aid to the country. France remains Morocco's closest trading partner and provides the country with extensive technical, financial, and educational aid, for which there is an urgent need. Relations with the Soviet Union are cordial and developing, and the USSR is a major purchaser of Moroccan phosphates.

Morocco also identifies with the aspirations of the Arab world, including the call for Arab unity, opposition to Zionism, pride in a common cultural, religious, historical, and linguistic heritage, and a desire to assert an authentic Arab identity. In addition, Morocco's ties to the Arab world have been an important source of economic assistance. Saudi Arabia in particular has provided Morocco with considerable financial aid in recent years, helping to offset the high cost of the war in the Western Sahara. At the same time, however, Morocco is less intensely involved in inter-Arab affairs than are the states of the Arab East. Indeed, Hassan, like Sadat when he ruled Egypt, has been particularly proud—some would say arrogant—about his country's independent stance on many controversial Middle East issues. Nowhere is this more evident than in Morocco's relationship with Israel, a relationship for which the king, reflecting both close personal and cultural ties with the West and a sensitivity to European public opinion, politicians, and pressure groups, has been much more willing to ignore, bypass, or contravene the Muslim consensus. The most recent and dramatic initiative in this regard took place in July 1986 in Ifrane, Morocco, when King Hassan met the Israeli Prime Minister, Shimon Peres, for discussions on the Palestinian question. The visit with the leader of the Arab world's most hated enemy, Israel, reflected Hassan's confidence about the national support that he commands on foreign policy issues. Most Moroccans feel a strong sense of pride in the country's leading role in major regional and international issues, although in the case of the Peres visit this pride was somewhat tempered by the recollection of the ultimate fate of Anwar Sadat; the pride was replaced by the awareness of the dangers inherent in such an initiative.

Pan-Arab feeling is widespread among both urban and rural groups in Moroccan society and is also a significant element in the political ideology of such parties as the Istiqlal and the USFP. The new urban-based middle classes feel a particularly strong affinity for their counterparts in the Middle East and thus a concern over the Arab-Israeli conflict. To such groups the danger of a schism between Morocco and the Arab world, on top of the diplomatic problems at the United Nations and in the Organization of African Unity caused by the Western Sahara conflict, has tended to dampen somewhat their sense of national pride over the king's bold gesture. Public reactions, however, have been reserved, with no overt demonstrations against the regime. Indeed, Arab criticisms from Syria and Libya, for example, have reinforced Moroccan support for the king, and the dissolution of the two-year-old Afro-Arab Federation with Libya in August 1986 was little regretted by most Moroccans.

On this, as on other issues dealing with Israel and Moroccan Jews, the king has remained steadfastly progressive, permitting native-born Moroccan Jews, for example, to feel secure in their futures by providing them with economic and even limited political opportunities. Yet, in all these initiatives, there is no sense of cultural consensus or even vague societywide support. Rather, a popular leader, acting mostly on his own, initiates foreign policy actions that have as much domestic political significance as they have impact on Morocco's regional and international standing. That is why many cynics and disaffected elements of the middle class who question the monarchy's legitimacy believe that the king's policies abroad are basically undertaken to mobilize support for the monarchy or to distract attention from pressing domestic problems. The examples that are so often cited to support such a view include Morocco's participation in the 1973 Arab-Israeli war, Hassan's decision in 1977 to send Moroccan paratroop units to Zaire to support Sese Seko Mobutu's struggle with secessionist forces, the launching of the Green March into the Western Sahara in 1975, and the Morocco-inspired union with Libya in August 1984.

Moroccan foreign policy would take a very different turn should modernist, messianic, or militarist elements replace monarchical power. In almost each instance, a replacement regime would seek to tie Morocco's behavior abroad much more closely to the Muslim consensus. As a result, overt political and symbolic ties to the West—France, the United States, Israel—would significantly decrease, although given the structural conditions inhibiting Moroccan economic choices, economic relations would only be marginally affected. In any case, short of a humiliating and disastrous military defeat in the Western Sahara or in combat against Algerians involved in that struggle (a diminished possibility since the reestablishment of diplomatic relations between Morocco and Algeria in May 1988), it seems unlikely that the fate of the Moroccan polity will be determined by foreign policy issues. In the final analysis the dominant monarchical culture will stand or fall on the basis of its ability to promote cultural synthesis, adaptive modernization, and incremental democratization within the Muslim consensus. Even the renewed interest in the idea of pan-Maghrebin unity, as reflected in the numerous contacts and agreements taking place between Algeria and Morocco, cannot undermine this fundamental reality. For their part, U.S. foreign policy decisionmakers must cultivate an attitude of "patient realism" (Lapidus 1983, 66) in dealing with a society undergoing fundamental social and economic change. Yet, unlike other Muslim societies in similar situations, Morocco's dilemmas are not cultural or religious in origin. They are thus amenable to resolution in a nonrevolutionary manner should enlightened leadership at home prevail and external allies remain supportive but noninterventionist.

Chapter Five

Cultural
Continuity
and Change

Socialization to politics, as part of a general cultural transmission from generation to generation, is a relatively continuous, nondisruptive process throughout much of Morocco. Nonetheless, major changes are under way, especially among large groups of rural migrants now living on the periphery of expansive cities. These urban malcontents, many rootless and alienated, poor and desperate, are culturally "afloat"; they are only tenuously connected to their traditional heritage, yet are incompletely socialized into the modern world. For the majority of Moroccans, however, change has been a dialectical rather than dichotomous experience, involving the incremental acquisition of new ideas and techniques in the context of traditional norms, ties, and loyalties. As has been noted earlier, Moroccans have moved and continue to move toward modern values and attitudes while remaining deeply impregnated with traditional beliefs (see Mernissi 1987).

SOCIALIZATION PATTERNS

Three broad yet distinct socialization patterns in Morocco involve incumbent and aspirant elites, the rural peasantry, and the urban masses. While all share common ties to the Muslim consensus, expressed with varying degrees of intensity, differing socialization experiences have produced distinct views of how power and politics should be articulated, organized, and applied.

Like their counterparts elsewhere in the Maghreb, Morocco's top elite are the product of "mixed" cultural influences and experiences—native and foreign, Arab and European, religious and secular. But unlike the case with other North African elites, many of these experiences have been fused in the period of a single generation. Thus, "some Moroccans underwent childhood socialization under the mahkzan, formal education under the French, and found career opportunities in the government of independent Morocco" (Waterbury 1970, 318). Elite political socialization in Morocco therefore is best understood as an experiential synthesis rather than as an insulated pocket of Europeanization achieved at the cost of cultural authenticity, as happened, for example, among so many *évolués* (superficially Europeanized members of the elite) in Algeria. Very few Moroccans, by comparison, have ever had to learn Arabic as a second language. This is not to imply, however, that Morocco's elites were or are like everyone else. Indeed, existing high social status is often linked to educational advantage and economic privilege to create a "ruling class" mentality. As Tessler correctly summarized:

[T]he values and behavioral norms of [Morocco's political elite] reflect their privileged background and near monopoly on preparation for national leadership. Those fortunate enough to have had the family connections and/or educational qual- ifications necessary to enter the leadership class at the outset have thereafter had a privileged position; and the result has been a small, ingrown and essentially closed elite that sees itself as the natural rulers of the nation and that makes at best a hazy distinction between its own interests and those of the country as a whole (1982, 71–72).

The generation that fought for political independence and assumed important leadership positions in the immediate post-1956 period shares common socializing experiences: Its members are of middle-class and upper-bourgeoisie background, educated in French secular schools in Morocco and at universities in France, bicultural and bilingual in orientation, partners in in- termarriage within established social and political circles, ben- eficiaries of monarchical rule and its system of patron-client relations, symbolically associated with the Muslim consensus (although personal motivation, along with a fascination with

French culture, civilization, and society, tends to dilute the full meaning of being a "good" Muslim), and virtually cut off from the rest of Moroccan society in regard to cultural ties and identities. Despite a temporary "bump" on the ideological spectrum during their university days, when left-wing and Marxist ideas seemed intellectually compelling or simply fashionable ("radical chic"), pre- and immediate postindependence elites are essentially conservative, status quo individuals sharing the same values and orientations as the rest of the urban bourgeoisie, whether in their capacity as the king's men or leaders of opposition parties and unions.

Although many of these elites resent the way in which political power at the top has been manipulated and abused, few are willing to give up their many privileges, a situation that would inevitably follow a transfer of power to a corruption-free republican leadership. Many observers have assumed that second and third generation elites, having grown up under this "corrupt" system, would be much less willing to cooperate in its continuation and, instead, would be the instruments for its rationalization and democratization. Yet the unchanging character of both political style and attitudes of successive generations has been one of the most striking features of Moroccan elite politics. One particularly astute student of Moroccan affairs, writing in the postscript of a highly regarded book (Leveau 1985), comments that, at first view, "one is struck by the continuity between Morocco of the 1960s and the Morocco of 1984. Thirty years after independence and despite two serious military coup attempts, the same independence-era political class is still in power" (245).

This suggests that, rhetoric and university experience aside, those individuals born to the ruling class come to share in the same values and expectations as their generational predecessors. Whatever else may be happening at the level of the subelites, along with the obvious major changes taking place among the urban masses, younger members of the ruling urban bourgeoisie as well as their social counterparts in the countryside, where landed notables have extensive and enduring ties to the throne, have become virtual replicas of their parents. Sons and daughters of the ruling elite who are in their twenties and thirties come from privileged background, are sent to French and U.S. universities, speak two or three foreign languages fluently, move easily in European and cosmopolitan social and cultural circles, and believe that they are best qualified to assume the mantle of leadership in the future. Unlike their parents and grandparents, however, the third and fourth generation of top elites-to-be are much more imbued with the Muslim consensus, which links them in a real way with Morocco's mass culture.

The prototype of this younger generation of elites is the crown prince himself, Sidi Mohamed. Although he has not been sent overseas for schooling, the twenty-five-year-old future king has been given a thoroughly European education while being brought up ostensibly as a devout Muslim, Arab, and Moroccan nationalist. Unlike his once flamboyant father, the young prince is serious (at least in public), conscientious, almost austere. At the many official functions that he is required to attend, he rarely smiles. He may not be the most personable individual at the palace, but Sidi Mohamed is gaining the respect and admiration of many Moroccans, including those usually opposed to the monarchy.

Where generational differences are having significant consequences, however, is at the level of second-tier and aspirant elites (see Sehimi 1988). Although the size and political orientation of the top elite have not changed radically since the 1960s, the same cannot be said for the emergent subelites. Because of the demographic explosion—Morocco's net birthrate approaches 4 percent per annum, one of the highest in the world—and a system of universal primary education, young Moroccan men and women are reaching working adulthood in unprecedented numbers. These people come from diverse social and geographic backgrounds. Many of them have flooded into the cities to attend secondary school or university at a time when the economy and polity are insufficiently equipped to satisfy people's high employment and social status expectations adequately. To this has been added the problem of a less-rigorous academic training associated with an all-Arabic curriculum that is not staffed with enough appropriately qualified instructors.

This phenomenon is particularly pronounced at the university level, where excess capacity has resulted in too many graduates with inadequate and inappropriate preparation, demanding prestigious positions and employment commensurate with what they believe a university graduate should command. A narrow political base and an unpredictable economy simply cannot absorb these numbers. The result is a very large segment of subelites-to-be frustrated and bitter about their personal and professional situations. Expectedly, their grievances have turned against the political system in general and the patrimonial elites in particular. This explains the wide attitudinal disjuncture evident between a precollegiate student population that shows strong support for the political system, its symbols and leaders (see Suleiman 1985) and the pervasive sense of political disaffection, cynicism, and alienation revealed by many university students (see Moore 1970; Palmer and Nedelcovych 1984; Nedelcovych and Palmer 1982; Nedelcovych 1980; and Moore and Hochschild 1968). It seems unlikely that the educational reforms announced in May 1987, intended to diminish this "overproduction," will have much impact in the near or intermediate future.

A socialization process originally intended to educate and train a manageable number of politically docile yet technically qualified subelite has simply been overwhelmed by a combination of demographic pressures and an educational explosion. The monarchical system has been able to absorb only a small minority of these people. For the rest, modernist, militarist, and, particularly, messianic formulations seem the only viable alternatives. In other words, educational frustrations, the lack of appropriate employment opportunities, and what is perceived as political sclerosis at the top are all challenging the dominant culture in very pronounced ways.

Several scholars have summarized the dire political implications of these developments (see Tessler 1982 and Micaud 1974), with particular focus on both the low end (the high school dropout) and top end (the university graduate) of the incipient elite ladder. Zartman provided a succinct profile of the generation caught in the absorption crisis:

> The fact that these [third and fourth generation subelites] often tend to be semieducated, traditionalist school-leavers, trained only in Arabic and more hostile than frustrated in

their feelings toward modernization, suggests that their reaction will be neo-traditionalist . . . , Islamic, populist, xenophobic. . . . It will be one of cynical radicals, suspicious of any leadership . . . , intolerant, impatient, and embittered over being excluded from the public benefits that private corruption make appear inexhaustible (1974, 484–485).

In the countryside, socialization to politics is a much less disruptive process. Village life remains insulated from the national-level intrigues of politics and politicians. More and more children from these rural settings are attending primary school, but relatively few go on to receive high school diplomas or enroll in university. The early school environment establishes a positive association between the Muslim consensus and the monarchy (see Suleiman 1985) and encourages a generally supportive cultural orientation among the majority of the population. That the central authorities have respected rural autonomy, which itself coheres with existing cultural norms, simply adds to the regime's legitimacy in the eyes of the peasantry (see Nellis 1983).

Like the monarchy and its rural notable clientele, Morocco's rural dwellers are strongly tied to traditions. As Miller has observed:

Conservatism dominates the approach [of rural dwellers] to the present. Strategies of environmental decision-making are based on known knowledge of the traditional agricultural environment; opportunities adaptive to local environment and society are acted upon. Schooling, service in the army, encounters with government officials, changes in market structures . . . these are dealt with as they occur, incrementally, with no particular pattern of change apparent [to the people themselves] (1984, 7).

Monarchical culture is best suited to this strategy of adaptive modernization and social incrementalism, as applied to Morocco's expansive village society. For both *malik* (king) and *fellah* (peasant), the nature of change in rural Morocco is best understood as a series of incremental, not revolutionary, steps. "Change is experimental and incremental; change is largely what [villagers and rural tribesmen] accept and accommodate within what they have known. Society's cooperative bent and the communal spirit in effect tempers change, and renders the present, as was the past, an experience determined by the group: no one thus far has forced change down their collective tribal throats" (Miller 1984, 193). This contrasts dramatically with the Iranian experience under the monarchy when the shah, unlike Hassan, imposed a top-down modernization that severely upset culture and society.

In Imlil, the small tribal Berber village in the High Atlas mountains that Miller studied, as in so many out-of-the-way Moroccan hamlets, villages, and rural enclaves, change is a "do-it-yourself affair, with little interference or direction from outside. Political affairs are regulated within the context of the Moroccan State, and the State is focused on events and processes outside and beyond the bled" (Miller 1984, 194).

Those individuals who leave the security and predictability of rural village life for opportunities in the cities are the ones most exposed to the dangers of contrasting cultural norms for which they are little prepared emotionally, psychologically, or culturally. The recently arrived but uneducated or minimally educated mountain tribesman or rural villager quickly confronts a world of challenges. The socialization process would probably be even more disruptive were it not for the continued presence of rural culture in the urban areas. Rapid population growth, economic decline in the countryside, and perceived and real employment opportunities in large cities in both Morocco and Europe have all forced greater and greater numbers of young people to strike out into a "brave new world." If the frustrated young people of the middle-level elites-to-be constitute the intellectual vanguard challenging monarchical culture and incumbent power, it is the swelling underclass of unemployed and unemployable who may one day furnish the fodder for revolutionary action.

As indicated earlier, these urban marginals living in the slums and bidonvilles of Casablanca, Tangier, and Rabat, for example, do not yet perceive their problems in explicitly political terms: They are too busy surviving. In this current stage, they are outside the political and cultural influence of any one group or tendency. When given the opportunity they will lash out in hurt, anger, and bitterness, as the bloody riots of 1981 and 1984 so visibly demonstrated. If any sentiment captures their imagination, it is that of Islamism. But the full political implications of this cultural association will be felt in the next, not the current, generation. Should the various components of the discontented incipient, intermediate, and nonelites converge into a culturally and politically integrated whole, the consequences for the current regime could be disastrous.

INSTITUTIONS

In Morocco today, modern institutions are replacing traditional ones as the principle arenas for political socialization. Specifically, three competitive institutional milieus serve as agents of political socialization in Morocco. The first consists of those institutions that promote identity with and support for the dominant monarchical culture, including the monarchy itself; state-run primary and secondary schools; the electronic media (radio and television, both run by the government); the government-controlled print media; officially sanctioned mosques and other religious bodies; business enterprises, corporate institutions and structures both public and private; the military, including the bulk of its officer corps; the comprehensive national and subnational governmental structure, including the cabinet, parliament, progovernment political parties, unions, and professional associations; and the entire regional and communal administration.

The second milieu includes those institutions that have "mixed" capacities, either instilling supportive images of the dominant culture (as in the case of the Western Sahara issue) or serving as the mediums for antigovernment sentiment (as on many political and economic issues). The most important of such institutions are universities, independent unions (labor, student, professional); the independent print media (newspapers, journals, reviews, magazines); maraboutic lodges and brotherhoods; and professional circles, clubs, and associations.

Finally there are institutional environments that serve as countercultural socialization agents, including the slums and bidonvilles of Morocco's largest cities; unauthorized mosques and other makeshift religious milieus, which bring together fundamentalist preachers espousing militant Islam; athletic, sports, and social clubs, which serve as the arenas for the development of bodies and minds in the name of some higher Islamic truth; and the generalized institutional settings within which urbanization, industrialization, and rapid social mobilization take place.

These various socializing institutions have created a somewhat inconsistent political culture, especially for the young lower-class ex-peasant living in urban slums. Uneducated and unsophisticated, he benefits little from the modernizing agents of change and is somewhat cynical of the traditional ones (the monarchy and the religious establishment, for example). Likewise, the mixed institutions require schooling and a level of political cognition that the resident of the bidonville simply does not possess. How effective have these differing socializing institutions been in promoting an integrative political culture, one consistent with the culture of the entire society?

Several progovernment structures serve interrelated functions intended to socialize and integrate current and future generations into an enduring acceptance of monarchical culture, values, and symbols. The schools and the media are the principle instruments for socializing, educating, and informing the mass public about politics. Other institutions utilized to advance monarchical culture include patronage structures in government and economy, which encourage cooperation and collaboration; symbolic structures (religious, foreign policy), which appeal to many in the countryside and the less sophisticated in the cities; and participatory structures such as the Chamber of Deputies, the cabinet, trade unions, student and professional associations, and political parties, which are increasingly serving real political purposes as part of the monarch's policy of incremental democratization.

Probably the most important of these participatory structures in recent years have been the subnational administrative units involved in advancing local-level political decisionmaking. Since the 1976 decentralization laws, for example, the *collectivités locales* have been given new powers and responsibilities (see

Nellis 1983). An attempt is being made, both by the palace and the Ministry of the Interior, to devolve greater administrative responsibilities to the 850 rural and urban communes—elective bodies that compete with the centralized hierarchy or local administration controlled by the interior ministry. It has been suggested that the recent increased importance given to the *collectivités locales* constitutes a form of "tutorial democracy" (Nellis 1983), which may presage a significant political evolution in the months and years ahead.

Should the "consensual" institutions fail to maintain or advance monarchical culture, the throne possesses key organizational instruments by which to orchestrate or control Moroccan political life. Specifically, the bureaucracy, the Ministry of the Interior (especially the Forces Auxiliaires and the Sûreté Nationale), the army including the Gendarmerie Royale, the royal cabinet, the judiciary, and the press and its propaganda arm can all serve the purpose of controlling and containing the political system.

For most Moroccans these five components of institutional progovernment socialization—education, patronage, symbols, participation, and control/containment—are exceptionally persuasive in promoting a monarchical cultural orientation.

Moroccan institutions having mixed socialization functions both temper the power and influence of state-sponsored socialization activites and cushion the regime against the disruptive consequences of anomic mass culture. In other words, university campuses, independent labor and student unions, the private sector press and other independent print media, groups of scholarly, academic, artistic, and journalistic associations, certain maraboutic brotherhoods, and elements of the army officer corps may challenge some of the assumptions of monarchical power and politics, but they also give support to the Muslim consensus—that cornerstone of monarchical culture—and advance modernist goals with which the throne is itself associated, albeit in a more incremental manner. This prevents society from polarizing into an elite-dominated monarchical system promoting cultural synthesis, adaptive modernization, and incremental democratization at the top while a deeply resentful anti-Western, all-Arabic, all-Islamic mass culture evolves at the bottom. These mixed institutions are therefore best understood as buffers, which mediate differences and constrain excesses at both ends while providing opportunity for autonomous action of a democratic sort. Unlike neighboring Algeria, Morocco is not a mass society, thanks in part to the role of mixed institutions.

Discontinuous political socialization in Morocco is most evident among those people trapped in city slums, wrenched from their traditional moorings, uneducated and therefore unprepared to assume productive jobs. Unmobilizable in any modern sense—they neither go to school nor hold down regular jobs—such people are extremely vulnerable to radical appeals of the Islamic fundamentalist type. To date these anomic individuals have been more of a social than a political problem; that is, although they may be involved in varied criminal acts, they are not part of any large revolutionary movement. Morocco does not yet have a situation where thousands of marginalized urban discontents are on the threshhold of leading a revolt against the throne in the manner of Iran in 1979.

INTERNATIONAL INFLUENCES

Morocco has been at the crossroads of different civilizations for centuries, so it is not unusual that the country has been able to integrate, in a relatively peaceful manner, many foreign ideas, customs, and practices within its own well-established value system. Extensive tourism, proximity to Spain, the presence of large groups of Moroccan students and workers in France and other parts of Europe, the relatively free flow of ideas as evidenced in the diversity of foreign journals, newspapers, books, and periodicals found in the country's kiosks, libraries, and bookstores, all help explain the relatively cosmopolitan character of Moroccan urban life. Additionally, the brevity of French and Spanish colonial rule—despite the continuing presence of the Spanish presidios of Ceuta and Melilla—has not left a bitter legacy of animosity and distrust toward all things European.

Western exposure and influence continue unabated, with tourism being an especially constant and pervasive form of intercultural contact, however superficial this may appear in some instances. For example, Agadir, along Morocco's southern Atlantic coast, has developed into an insulated enclave for European package tours that has very little significant impact on Moroccan society as a whole. Yet Agadir is the exception: Marrakesh, Casablanca, Fez, Meknes, Tangier, and Rabat are more representative examples of how international influences have been harmoniously adapted into Moroccan culture.

This is not to suggest, however, that there has not been a cultural backlash among certain groups in society to the more blatant aspects of European social behavior. For many newly settled slum dwellers of Casablanca, for example, there is a simultaneous attraction to and reaction against the sight of European female topless bathers at Morocco's beaches and pools. Likewise, European tourist enclaves of the Club Med type offend many members of the more traditional segments of society. Yet, unlike the situation in neighboring Algeria, there has not yet developed a movement of fundamentalist "guardians of morality" who attack tourist hotels, public beaches, cabarets, night clubs, and other centers of "infidel evil." This may yet happen, but if it does, it will not find great support among most Moroccans.

Beyond these more outward instances of intercultural accommodation are the substantive examples of Western ideas and democratic principles seeping into Moroccan culture. By most Afro-Arab standards, Moroccan intellectual, academic, journalistic, and literary life is exceptionally liberal, with only intermittent instances of government crackdown against certain publications or political figures espousing explicitly antigovernment ideas. Moreover, many of these forums for open political discourse are not limited to European-language media, which, in any case, would be relevant to only a relatively small minority of Moroccan people. Instead, Arabic-language writings, for which there is a relatively sizable audience, are also permitted to express fairly contentious points of view. That the monarchy is often in the forefront of encouraging such liberalism further legitimizes the role of certain Western concepts among groups of people who might otherwise be put off or offended by nontraditional beliefs or practices.

In the political sphere as well, democratic processes such as political party competition, campaigning, elections, and parliamentary debates, many of which have been borrowed directly from the West, have now become regular features of Moroccan national politics however much the throne attempts to interfere or manipulate the outcomes of such processes.

In summary, the influence of foreign ideas, contacts, and experiences, including extensive economic ties with the outside world, have all been part of a long-term historical process. Moroccan culture has been particularly adept at integrating these influences without undermining or uprooting its own values and beliefs. To be sure, culture in Morocco has changed "amidst various international ideological clashes as well as continuing capitalistic penetration and Western cultural influences" (Joseph and Joseph 1987, 10). Yet, despite these influences and penetrations and in the face "of the astonishing power of a world culture bent on making all lesser entities subservient to its master logic" (Joseph and Joseph 1987, 25), Morocco's cultural core remains alive and vital.

In the more modern period, the extensive types and levels of intercultural exchanges have been transformed both into economic payoffs (tourism, for example) and into political role models from which democratic tendencies in the country have been molded. These tendencies have checked, albeit modestly, the authoritarian excesses often exhibited by the monarchy. This interactive process has influenced the top elite as much as those immediately below them. The countryside has remained solidly committed to its traditional values for which external ideas remain just that—external.

It is among the mushrooming group of discontented underclass on the periphery of Moroccan urban life that the appropriateness and long-term durability of Western ideas, contacts, and practices remain problematic. To date, young unemployed males from the slums simply harass both foreign and native women sporting bikinis or less on Morocco's many tourist beaches and pools. In the future, however, that harassment could escalate into something more socially or politically ominous.

This development will have to be watched carefully in the years ahead, for it has serious implications for the viability of the cultural synthesis, adaptive modernization, and incremental democratization upon which so much of the regime's legitimacy is based.

Chapter Six

Culture, Counterculture, and Politics: Summary and Forecasts

There are no permanent cultural "exiles" or "enemies" in Morocco and, therefore, no full-fledged counterculture. For example, the country has no counterpart to the Arabs in Israel, blacks in South Africa, or Bahais in Iran. Even Morocco's dwindling Jewish community, although insecure, is not an outcast or target of physical abuse or persecution. Yet culturally based opposition does exist, and it is capable of being transformed into an incipient counterculture, not unlike a similar phenomenon observable in Tunisia over the past decade and a half (see Entelis 1974).

The most likely source of political opposition at home comes from the existing (sub)cultures, which can cooperate, compete, or conflict with the dominant monarchical culture. At one time or another the following groups have turned against the regime: the liberal and *gauchiste* modernists, elements of the military, and Islamic fundamentalists. The scope and intensity of organized opposition have normally been manageable, although the two unsuccessful assassination attempts by the military against the king in 1971 and 1972 were very close calls. Unorganized and spontaneous revolts by slum dwellers, workers, and students have uncertain cultural roots but no ideological focus. The only exception to the above are the extremists on the left who are found almost exclusively in Europe. Marxists reject completely the monarchist policy of incrementalism, seeking, instead, a total cultural reordering of society. Although such groups constitute an authentic counterculture, they are politically insignificant.

As has been noted several times earlier, Muslim messianic tendencies come closest to constituting a counterculture of some import. Playing down the Arab and Moroccan dimensions of the Muslim consensus, fundamentalists emphasize the role of Islam—pure and pristine—as the sole expression of personal and popular will. Such a populist Islam of the poor continues to attract large numbers of people at Morocco's social periphery. As we have seen, militant Islam invokes increased individual piety as well as the expression of dissatisfaction with socioeconomic inequalities.

The political significance of Islamic protest movements lies in two areas. First, much of the increased religious consciousness reflects both discontent with present economic and political conditions and a belief that modern politics is linked to bourgeois privilege and the exploitation of the masses in contemporary Morocco. The current Islamic revival signifies a direct opposition to the prevailing political order. Second, the religious revival expands the following and influence of Islamic personalities and organizations outside the religious establishment, some of which are strongly opposed to the present government.

The real danger to incumbent authority is that unknown numbers of Muslim activists are members of the military, the police, and the civil service; this is similar to what has developed in Egypt since the assassination of Anwar Sadat by Muslim zealots in October 1981. Some scholars argue that militants in key institutional settings, in conjunction with student groups and other disaffected elements in the cities and the countryside, may one day become a force that could assume political power if the monarchy should falter or the military establishment be overthrown.

As long as protest movements remain rooted in policy or personality differences, not cultural ones, the monarchy has the inherent capacity to counter any challenges to its rule effectively. At the broadest level, the king has successfully expropriated the culturally related symbols of Islamic legitimacy to himself and his throne. At the operational level, a carrot-and-stick policy has often been sufficient to contain dissidents and reward compliers. If these measures should prove insufficient, the monarch always has available the combination of "agenda control, cooptation, and orchestration" (Zartman 1987, 25) to enforce compliance of those unconvinced of the king's *baraka* or indifferent to his blandishments. Keeping friends and foes alike "busy, dependent, and divided" (Zartman 1987, 18) has long been a favorite tactic of royal orchestration.

Should all else fail, of course, the monarchy has the monopoly of coercive force in the state to ensure ultimate obedience. It is remarkable, however, that this extreme form of system compliance has not been employed nearly so frequently as circumstances in which its use could have been justified might indicate. In this regard Morocco is no repressive state in which government violence and force are used indiscriminately; state violence and control "operate along side and not as an alternative" (Zartman 1987, 25) to the co-optation and orchestration associated with monarchical rule. State violence in Morocco "is neither constant nor capricious, but rather reactive and purposive. It responds to cyclical sources of violence on the part of the opposition outside or on the edges of the polity and it also adopts its own rhythms of repression and relaxation geared to other events on its schedule" (Zartman 1987, 25).

It is in the context of repression and reform that the monarchy seeks to contain challenges to its authority. Whether originating from dissident army officers, radical university students, left-wing militants, discontented laborers, Muslim zealots, or simply urban malcontents, political opposition in Morocco has yet to spill over into the system's cultural core. When royal orchestration and co-optation have appeared inadequate, the state could always employ its broad coercive capacities. During the 1970s, for example, the use of state violence accomplished a number of purposes: "[I]t established and repeatedly reasserted the left boundary of the polity; it removed a generation of dedicated opponents in the ranks of both the students and the military; it warned their successors to be a little bit more understanding; it kept up pressure on the UNFP/USFP to make it more manageable and to join in the policy of cooptation; [and] it was effective in reasserting state control" (Zartman 1987, 27).

While opposition to the regime in the 1980s has become more diffused—disparate groups of the unemployed, religious zealots, high school and university students—government response has remained consistent (repression and reform), without any guarantees, however, that similar challenges will not reemerge in the future.

Despite the persistence and at times the severity of anti-government behavior in the form of riots, demonstrations, strikes, coup attempts, and the like, Moroccan society seems unprepared for radical cultural change. Simultaneously, however, the monarchy's policies of cultural synthesis, adaptive modernization, and incremental democratization have not yet taken sufficient hold at the national level to ensure system legitimacy in the long run. Possibly more disturbing for many citizens are the cruel intricacies of Moroccan politics, a special Arab blend of personal feuds and shifting alliances, of sudden "fraternity" and equally sudden denunciation. In the final analysis it is this unpredictability that disenchants so many in Morocco today and that one day may find expression in a system-threatening political counterculture.

A culturally based analysis of Morocco reveals a political system capable of reconciling traditional beliefs with modern practices while advancing incremental forms of political participation. As this study has shown, culture in Morocco is forged by a dialectical and interactive relationship between the specific traditions of Islam, Arabim, and Moroccan history and identity—the Muslim consensus—and the canons of a spreading scientific and material world culture. Perceptions of these alternatives and suitability vary over time and are affected by changing world conditions. The modern civilization of Morocco is forged by gradual and evolutionary processes of cultural synthesis, adaptive modernization, and incremental democratization. Although monarchical culture currently dominates, it is often challenged by modernist, militarist, and messianic subcultures, which also adhere to the Muslim consensus but dispute the appropriateness and pace of the regime's policies of cultural synthesis, adaptive modernization, and incremental democratization.

Monarchical culture in Morocco confirms the notion that secularization is not a prerequisite for the attainment of the distinctive characteristics of the modern state (Carroll 1984, 364). If the core character of political modernity is the "existence of a very extensive capacity to undertake large, complex tasks on a regular and continuing basis" (Carroll 1984, 371), then clearly Morocco must be considered politically modern. It possesses extensive capacities in the areas of communication, coercion, legitimation, planning, and policy implementation that are the hallmarks of modern state systems (Carroll 1984, 371). A society like Morocco's, with a traditional cultural core—the Muslim consensus—is very much capable of obtaining these five political capabilities. In sum, culture and politics in Morocco interact in a relatively harmonious manner, providing purpose and direction for people and politics. Unlike so many societies in the Third World that are caught in painful transition between a traditional order fractured beyond effective repair and a yet-to-be-created modern entity, Morocco has functionally blended continuity and change.

Given this significant advantage denied other transitional societies, King Hassan has a historic opportunity to transform his broadly based cultural support into a viable, institutionally pluralistic system of rule that his son, Crown Prince Sidi Mohamed, can inherit and advance. If, however, the opportunity is wasted and arbitration rather than leadership continues to guide political life, then the monarchy's future is problematic. Ultimately, if the monarchy is overthrown, no single counter-cultural component or remnant of the nonroyal incumbent elites could mobilize all three pillars of the Muslim consensus. The result would be chronic instability, violence, and insecurity both for the country and for the North African region as a whole.

In light of the above analysis, what are Morocco's political options for the future? Five alternative regimes based on some-what different cultural constituencies are identifiable, each discussed in descending order of likelihood for the near (one-to-three-year) and intermediate (three-to-five-year) future.

The most likely regime for the first half of the 1990s is that of the current monarchy, the three-hundred-year-old Alawite dynasty. As we have seen, King Hassan faces several threats, some of which might become serious if socioeconomic conditions worsen or if the country suffers a major defeat in the Sahara war. Challenges to the king's rule come from Muslim funda-mentalists, university and high school students, labor unions, leftist parties, intellectuals and journalists, and the bulk of the urban underclass. But these groups do not represent a cohesive cultural force able to organize an overthrow of the monarchy.

The monarch is the center of real power, disbursing patronage and balancing the demands of political parties, labor unions, newspapers, radio and television, security organizations, and the military. King Hassan strives to make sure that there are as many political parties as possible, and that no single group becomes too strong or too weak.

The king is supported by the armed forces, which are being strengthened in their Sahara campaign. Although the country has suffered a series of diplomatic defeats regarding the Western Sahara (seventy countries currently recognize the Sahrawi Arab Democratic Republic—SADR), its military performance in the field has improved dramatically with the completion of the sixth desert "wall." The king also has the backing of rural Berber notables, the business community, and the bureaucracy, who depend on him for their livelihood. Challenges from the POLISARIO and diplomatic opposition from Algeria are counterbalanced by the strong commitment of the United States and France to increase military and economic aid to the kingdom. The on-again, off-again experiment in democratization seems to be on again, especially at the subnational level. Despite the current social and economic problems, the king still has ample support from a broad range of the population who believe the monarchy is the fourth pillar of the Muslim consensus. All this ensures a continuation of his regime for the near and intermediate future. In the event of the king's death, his son the crown prince, would succeed him, unless a coup overthrew the monarchy.

The second most likely regime would be that of a right-wing military junta that would achieve power through a military coup or in the aftermath of the physical liquidation of monarchy, monarch, and royal successors. The military generally opposes change; nevertheless it is the greatest source of threat to the current regime. As we have seen, the army is guided by a narrow-minded praetorian culture that is uncomfortable with genuine democracy and social change.

Threats from the military may be moderated by their memories of the consequences of the failed coups of 1971, 1972, and 1983, and because the monarchy is preferable to any possible alternative government formed by political parties and union leadership. The presence of informers and secret police among the military helps to assure the loyalty of the troops. In addition, the recent improvement in Morocco's military position in the war has raised army morale.

Yet the possibility of a military coup d'état should not be ruled out, since most of the conditions that spurred high-level Berber officers' attempts to take power in the early 1970s and, most recently, in early 1983, are still in evidence, including corruption elsewhere in the military and in the civilian elite. Some military men, especially younger junior officers, may be disturbed, from a religious and moral viewpoint, by the apparent decadence of the Hassan regime. More than any particular developments abroad or in the Sahara war except a massive and humiliating military defeat, the desire for moral rectitude and organizational efficiency in the face of a steadily decaying socioeconomic order might one day force the military to take matters into their own hands. Such a regime would not have a broad base of popular support and would therefore not overturn existing government policies but would seek to eliminate the weaknesses in the government.

The third most likely regime would be that of a "liberal democracy" on the model of Spain under Juan Carlos. Such a regime would represent the liberal wing of modernist culture and would emerge from a confluence of party, union, professional, business, and enlightened military groupings. The king himself could institute such a regime in incremental stages, or a military coup could establish the conditions for its establishment, as happened in neighboring Tunisia with the "constitutional" coup of November 7, 1987, which saw the removal of the "royalist" president, Habib Bourguiba. In any case a liberal modernist regime would symbolically identify with the Muslim consensus but be vigorous in its implementation of genuinely free elections, party and union activity, a free press, and a decisionmaking parliament. The liberal professions, elements of the bureaucracy, and the West would all welcome such a regime. There is no evidence to date, however, that Hassan is voluntarily moving in this liberal direction at a pace sufficient to satisfy those representing modernist culture.

A puritanical, fundamentalist movement, supported by militant students, workers, and junior officers, would be a fourth most likely alternative regime to the current monarchy. Students and workers in Casablanca and other large Moroccan cities as well as a small but radical band of Islamic fundamentalists took to the streets in 1978, 1979, 1981, and, most violently, in January 1984, to demonstrate for economic and political goals. They do not speak with one voice, but they all oppose the present regime.

The protest groups are part of a broader category of youths, intellectuals, students, representatives of the lower-middle class, and elements of the urban underclass that would like to see Islam restored and transformed into a new set of principles to help the people find original solutions to the crises around them. Among these groups, a certain element, especially in the countryside, in the Rif, or in the Middle Atlas regions, may join conservative fundamentalist organizations whose influence spreads beyond the limits of North Africa. Many in the opposition may seek some radical fundamentalist movement that would rebuild a stronger Moroccan community. Should all these forces coalesce—very unlikely at this point—they would constitute a powerful force that might seriously challenge both the monarchy and the military system that supports it. Once in power, the fundamentalist-led radicals would reverse all major domestic and foreign policies of the current government and institute a more Islamic and nationalistic system of rule.

The fifth and least likely regime to replace the incumbent government would emerge from a *gauchiste*-modernist culture. Representing extremist left-wing and Marxist tendencies found among students, workers, and intellectuals in Europe and Morocco, a *gauchiste* regime would abolish the monarchy, push for socialist solutions to economic and social problems, and redirect Moroccan foreign policy toward the socialist and Third Worlds, while paying lip service to the Muslim consensus. Extreme left-wing tendencies espousing secular and revolutionary programs have limited popular support and no apparent ties to military groups, which would be needed to overthrow the monarchy. Even in the wake of total social anarchy and political breakdown, it seems very unlikely that radical socialist forces could pick up the pieces of national leadership.

More so than ever before, Morocco is at a crucial juncture due to its exposure to international pressures and deep socioeconomic problems. Nevertheless, as this study has argued, the country's "cultural harmony" (Leveau 1985, 277) may yet enable it to overcome these multiple challenges in a nonviolent manner. It is clear that past political practices of ruling through limited coteries of co-opted elites can no longer be considered a viable option, for, unlike the colonization and decolonization processes, current socioeconomic and demographic problems may significantly alter Morocco's "deep structures" (Leveau 1985, 277).

References and Bibliography

Abu-Lughod, Janet L., 1979. "Dependent Urbanism and Decolonization: The Moroccan Case." *Arab Studies Quarterly* 1 (1, Winter): 49–66.

———. 1980. *Rabat: Urban Apartheid in Morocco*. Princeton, N.J.: Princeton University Press.

Abun-Nasr, Jamil M. 1975. *A History of the Maghrib*. Cambridge, UK: Cambridge University Press.

———. 1987. *A History of the Maghrib in the Islamic Period*. Cambridge: Cambridge University Press.

Almond, Gabriel A., and Sidney Verba, eds. 1980. *The Civic Culture Revisited*. Boston: Little, Brown.

Al Amin, Ahmed. 1968. "L'évolution de la femme et le problème du mariage au Maroc." *Présence Africaine* 68:32–51.

Amin, Samir. 1970. *The Maghreb in the Modern World: Algeria, Tunisia, Morocco*. Baltimore, Md.: Penguin Books.

Ammar, Hamed. 1966. *Growing Up in an Egyptian Village: Silwa, Province of Aswan*. New York: Octagon Books.

Ashford, Douglas E. 1959. "Politics and Violence in Morocco." *Middle East Journal* 13 (1): 11–25.

———. 1961a. *Political Change in Morocco*. Princeton, N.J.: Princeton University Press.

———. 1961b. "Political Usage of 'Islam' and 'Arab Culture.'" *Public Opinion Quarterly* 25 (1): 106–114.

———. 1964. *Perspectives of a Moroccan Nationalist*. Totowa, N.J.: The Bedminster Press.

———. 1973. "Second- and Third-Generation Elites in the Maghrib." In I. William Zartman, ed., *Man, State, and Society in the Contemporary Maghrib*. New York: Praeger.

Barakat, Halim, ed. 1985. *Contemporary North Africa: Issues of Development and Integration.* Washington, D.C.: Center for Contemporary Arab Studies.

Barbier, Maurice. 1982. *Le conflit du Sahara Occidental.* Paris: L'Harmattan.

Beau, Nicolas. July 12, 1984. "Etre jeune au Maghreb: Maroc—entre le ballon et le Coran." *Le Monde* (Paris).

Ben-Dor, Gabriel. 1977. "Political Culture Approach to Middle East Politics." *International Journal of Middle East Studies* 8 (1, January): 43–63.

Berger, Morroe. 1964. *The Arab World Today.* New York: Doubleday-Anchor Books.

Bernard, Stephane. 1968. *The Franco-Moroccan Conflict, 1943–1956.* New Haven, Conn.: Yale University Press.

Berque, Jacques. 1967. *French North Africa: The Maghrib Between the Two World Wars.* London: Faber and Faber.

————. 1973. "Tradition and Innovation in the Maghrib." *Daedalus* 102 (1, Winter): 239–250.

————. 1978. *Cultural Expression in Arab Society Today.* Austin, Tex.: University of Texas Press.

Berque, Jacques, and Jean-Paul Charnay. 1967. *L'Ambivalence dans la Culture Arabe.* Paris: Editions Anthropos.

Berrada, Mohamed. 1985. "The New Cultural and Imaginative Discourse in Morocco: Utopic Change." In Halim Barakat, ed., *Contemporary North Africa: Issues of Development and Integration.* Washington, D.C.: Georgetown University Center for Contemporary Arab Studies.

Bill, James, and Carl Leiden. 1984. *Politics in the Middle East.* Boston: Little, Brown.

Binder, Leonard. 1969. "Egypt: The Integrative Revolution." In Lucian W. Pye and Sidney Verba, eds., *Political Culture and Political Development.* Princeton, N.J.: Princeton University Press.

Bouanami, Ahmed. 1966. "Introduction à la poésie populaire marocaine." *Souffles* 3:3–9.

Boukous, Ahmed. 1977. *Langage et Cultures Populaires au Maroc.* Casablanca: Imprimeries Dar El-Kitab.

Braun, Frank H. 1978. "Morocco: Anatomy of a Palace Revolution that Failed." *International Journal of Middle East Studies* 9:63–72.

Brett, Michael. 1978. "Islam in the Maghreb: The Problem of Modernization." *Maghreb Review* 3 (5-6): 6–9.

Brown, Kenneth L. 1976. *People of Salé: Tradition and Change in a Moroccan City, 1830–1930.* Cambridge, Mass.: Harvard University Press.

Brown, Leon Carl. 1966. "The Role of Islam in Modern North Africa." In Leon Carl Brown, ed., *State and Society in Independent North Africa.* Washington, D.C.: Middle East Institute.

Burke, Edmund, III. 1972. "The Image of the Moroccan State in French Ethnological Literature: A New Look at the Origin of Lyautey's Berber Policy." In Ernest Gellner and Charles Micaud, eds., *Arabs and Berbers: From Tribe to Nation in North Africa.* Lexington, Mass.: Lexington Books.

––––––. 1976. *Prelude to Protectorate in Morocco: Precolonial Protest and Resistance, 1860–1912.* Chicago: The University of Chicago Press.

Camau, Michel. 1971. *La Notion de Démocratie dans la Pensée des Dirigeants Maghrebins.* Paris: Centre National de la Recherche Scientifique.

Carroll, Terrance G. 1984. "Secularization and States of Modernity." *World Politics* 36 (3, April): 362–382.

––––––. 1986. "Islam and Political Community in the Arab World." *International Journal of Middle East Studies* 18:185–204.

Chaoui, Mohamed. 1978. "Sefrou: De la tradition à l'intégration, ce qu'est un petit centre d'aujourd'hui." *Lamalif* 99:32–39.

Charhadi, Driss Ben Hamed. 1964. *A Life Full of Holes.* Recorded and Translated by Paul Bowles. New York: Grove Press.

Chraibi, Farid. 1981. "Le 'Processus Democratique' au Maroc." *Les Temps Modernes* 417 (April): 1736–1763.

Clement, Jean-François. 1986. "Morocco's Bourgeoisie: Monarchy, State and Owning Class." *MERIP Report* 16 (5, September-October): 13–17.

Cohen, Mark I., and Lorna Hahn. 1966. *Morocco: Old Land, New Nation.* New York: Praeger.

Combs-Schilling, Elaine. 1982. "Meaning in the Midst of Change: Islam in Morocco." Unpublished Paper.

––––––. 1989. *Sacred Performances: Islam and Political Authority in Moroccan Resistance to Western Domination.* New York: Columbia University Press.

Coon, Carleton. 1934. *The Riffian.* London: Cape.

Crapanzano, Vincent. 1973. *The Hamadsha; A Study in Moroccan Ethnopsychiatry.* Berkeley, Calif.: University of California Press.

––––––. 1980. *Tuhami: Portrait of a Moroccan.* Chicago: University of Chicago Press.

Crawford, R. W. 1965. "Cultural Change and Communications in Morocco." *Human Organisation* 24 (1): 73–77.

Damis, John. 1970. "Developments in Morocco under the French Protectorate, 1925–1943." *The Middle East Journal* 24 (1, Winter): 74–86.

———. 1972. "The Moroccan Political Scene." *The Middle East Journal* 26 (1, Winter): 25–36.

———. 1973. "Early Moroccan Reactions to the French Protectorate: The Cultural Dimension." *Humaniora Islamica* 1:15–31.

———. 1975. "Morocco: Political and Economic Prospects." *The World Today* 31 (1, January): 36–46.

———. 1983. *Conflict in Northwest Africa: The Western Sahara Dispute*. Stanford, Calif.: Hoover Institution Press.

———. 1986. "Les Relations des Etats-Unis avec le Maroc." *Maghreb-Machrek* 111 (January-February-March): 5–23.

Davis, Susan Schaefer. 1978. "Working Women in a Moroccan Village." In Lois Beck and Nikki Keddie, eds., *Women in the Muslim World*. Cambridge, Mass.: Harvard University Press.

———. 1983. *Patience and Power: Women's Lives in a Moroccan Village*. Cambridge, Mass.: Schenkman Publishing.

Dejeux, Jean. 1985. *Poètes marocains de langue française*. Paris: Saint-Germain-des-Prés.

———. 1986. *Le sentiment religieux dans la littérature maghrébine de langue française*. Paris: L'Harmattan.

Dugas, Guy. 1987. "L'Edition au Maroc: livres et revues en langue française." *Maghreb-Machrek* 118 (October-November-December): 114–121.

Dunn, Ross E. 1977. *Resistance in the Desert: Moroccan Responses to French Imperialism, 1881–1912*. Madison, Wis.: University of Wisconsin Press.

Dwyer, Daisy. 1976. "Cultural Conceptions of Conflict and Variability in Conflict Boundaries." *Journal of Conflict Resolution* 20:663–680.

Dwyer, Daisy Hilse. 1978a. *Images and Self-Images: Male and Female in Morocco*. New York: Columbia University Press.

———. 1978b. "Women, Sufism, and Decision-Making in Moroccan Islam." In Lois Beck and Nikki Keddie, eds., *Women in the Muslim World*. Cambridge, Mass.: Harvard University Press.

Dwyer, Kevin. 1982. *Moroccan Dialogues: Anthropology in Question*. Baltimore, Md.: The Johns Hopkins Press.

Eickelman, Dale F. 1976. *Moroccan Islam: Tradition and Society in a Pilgrimage Center*. Austin, Tex.: University of Texas Press.

————. 1977. "Ideological Change and Regional Cults: Maraboutism and Ties of Closeness in Western Morocco." In R. P. Werbner, ed., *Regional Cults*. London: Academic Press.

————. 1978. "The Art of Memory: Islamic Education and its Social Reproduction." *Comparative Studies in Society and History* 20: (4): 485–516.

————. 1981. *The Middle East: An Anthropological Approach*. Englewood Cliffs, N.J.: Prentice-Hall.

————. 1985. *Knowledge and Power in Morocco: The Education of a Twentieth Century Notable*. Princeton, N.J.: Princeton University Press.

————. 1986. "Royal Authority and Religious Legitimacy: Morocco's Elections, 1960–1984." In Myron J. Aronoff, ed., *The Frailty of Authority*. New Brunswick, N.J.: Transaction Books.

Entelis, John P. 1974. "Ideological Change and an Emerging Counter-Culture in Tunisian Politics." *The Journal of Modern African Studies* 12 (4): 543–568.

————. 1975. "Reformist Ideology in the Arab World: The Cases of Tunisia and Lebanon." *The Review of Politics* 37 (4, October): 513–546.

————. 1980a. *Comparative Politics of North Africa: Algeria, Morocco, and Tunisia*. Syracuse, N.Y.: Syracuse University Press.

————. 1980b. "Kingdom of Morocco." In David E. Long and Bernard Reich, eds., *The Government and Politics of the Middle East and North Africa*. Boulder, Colo.: Westview Press.

————. 1981. "Elite Political Culture and Socialization in Algeria: Tensions and Discontinuities." *The Middle East Journal* 35 (2, Spring): 191–208.

————. 1985. "The Political Economy of North African Relations: Cooperation or Conflict?" In Halim Barakat, ed., *Contemporary North Africa: Issues of Development and Integration*. Washington, D.C.: Georgetown University Center for Contemporary Arab Studies.

————. 1986. *Algeria: The Revolution Institutionalized*. Boulder, Colo.: Westview Press.

Escallier, Robert. 1982. "Le système urbain marocain: métropoles et petites villes." *Maghreb-Machrek* 96 (April-May-June): 19–40.

Etienne, Bruno. 1983. "La Moelle de la Prédication: Essai sur le Prône Politique dans l'Islam Contemporain." *Revue Française de Science Politique* 33 (4, August): 700–709.

————. 1987. *L'Islamisme Radical*. Paris: Hachette.

Etienne, Bruno, and Mohamed Tozy. 1979. "Le glissement des obligations Islamiques vers le phénomène associatif à Casablanca." *Annuaire de L'Afrique du Nord* 18:235–259.

Findlay, Anne M., Allan M. Findlay, and Richard I. Lawless, compilers. 1984. *Morocco.* World Bibliographical Series, 47. Santa Barbara, Calif.: CLIO Press.

Foster, Stephen William. 1986. Review of Dale F. Eickelman, *Knowledge and Power in Morocco. The Middle East Journal* 40 (2, Spring): 363–364.

Gallagher, Charles F. 1963. *The United States and North Africa: Morocco, Algeria, and Tunisia.* Cambridge, Mass.: Harvard University Press.

———. 1967. "Language, Culture, and Ideology: The Arab World." In Kalman H. Silvert, ed., *Expectant Peoples: Nationalism and Development.* New York: Vintage Books.

Geertz, Clifford. 1968. *Islam Observed: Religious Development in Morocco and Indonesia.* New Haven, Conn.: Yale University Press.

———. 1973. *The Interpretation of Cultures.* New York: Basic Books.

———. 1976. "Art as a Cultural System." *Modern Language Notes* 91:1473–1499.

Geertz, Clifford, Hildred Geertz, and Lawrence Rosen. 1979. *Meaning and Order in Moroccan Society: Three Essays in Cultural Analysis.* Cambridge, UK: Cambridge University Press.

Gellner, Ernest. 1969. *Saints of the Atlas.* Chicago: University of Chicago Press.

———. 1972a. "Patterns of Tribal Rebellion in Morocco." In P. J. Vatikiotis, ed., *Revolution in the Middle East and Other Case Studies.* London: Allen & Unwin.

———. 1972b. "Introduction." In Ernest Gellner and Charles Micaud, eds., *Arabs and Berbers: From Tribe to Nation in North Africa.* Lexington, Mass.: Lexington Books.

Gellner, Ernest, and Charles Micaud, eds. 1972. *Arabs and Berbers: From Tribe to Nation in North Africa.* Lexington, Mass.: Lexington Books.

Gellner, Ernest, and John Waterbury, eds. 1977. *Patrons and Clients in Mediterranean Societies.* London: Duckworth.

Gillespie, Kate, and Gwenn Okruhlik. 1988. "Cleaning Up Corruption in the Middle East." *The Middle East Journal* 42 (1, Winter): 59–82.

Gilsenan, Michael. 1982. *Recognizing Islam: Religion and Society in the Modern Arab World.* New York: Pantheon Books.

Gordon, David C. 1962. *North Africa's French Legacy, 1954–1962.* Cambridge, Mass.: Harvard University Center for Middle Eastern Studies.

Grandguillaume, Gilbert. 1979. "Langue, identité et culture nationale au Maghreb." *Mediterranean Peoples* 9 (October-December): 3–28.

———. 1983. *Arabisation et politique linguistique au Maghreb.* Paris: Maisonneuve et Larose.

Hagopian, Elaine. 1967. "Conceptual Stability, the Monarchy and Modernization in Morocco." *Journal of Developing Areas* 1 (2, January): 199–214.

Halpern, Manfred. 1963. *The Politics of Social Change in the Middle East and North Africa.* Princeton, N.J.: Princeton University Press.

Halstead, John P. 1967. *Rebirth of a Nation: The Origins and Rise of Moroccan Nationalism, 1912–1944.* Cambridge, Mass.: Harvard University Middle East Monograph Series.

Hart, David Montgomery. 1976. *The Aith Waryaghar of the Moroccan Rif: An Ethnography and History.* Tucson, Ariz.: The University of Arizona Press.

Hasnaoui, Ahmed. 1977. "Certain Notions of Time in Arab-Muslim Philosophy." In H. Aguessy, ed., *Time and the Philosophies,* 49–79. Paris: Unesco Press.

Hazen, William E. 1979. "Minorities in Assimilation: The Berbers of North Africa." In R. D. McLaurin, ed., *The Political Role of Minority Groups in the Middle East.* New York: Praeger.

Hermassi, Elbaki. 1972. *Leadership and National Development in North Africa: A Comparative Study.* Berkeley, Calif.: University of California Press.

———. 1984. "La Société Tunisienne au Miroir Islamiste." *Maghreb Machrek* 103:39–56.

Hodges, Tony. 1983. *Western Sahara: The Roots of a Desert War.* Westport, Conn.: Lawrence Hill and Company.

Hoffman, Bernard G. 1967. *The Structure of Traditional Moroccan Rural Society.* The Hague: Mouton and Co.

Howard-Merriam, Kathleen. 1984. "Women's Political Participation in Morocco's Development: How Much and For Whom?" *The Maghreb Review* 9 (1-2): 12–23.

Ihrai, Said. 1986. *Pouvoir et Influence: Etat, Partis et Politique Etrangère au Maroc.* Rabat: Edino.

Joseph, Roger. 1980. "Toward a Semiotics of Middle Eastern Cultures." *International Journal of Middle East Studies* 12:319–329.

Joseph, Roger, and Terri Brint Joseph. 1987. *The Rose and the Thorn: Semiotic Structures in Morocco*. Tucson, Ariz.: The University of Arizona Press.

Kabbaj, Mohammed Mostafa. 1979. "Traditional Child Socialization and the Incursion of Mass Communication in Morocco." *International Social Science Journal* 31 (3): 429–443.

Karpat, Kemal H. 1986. "Nation and Nationality in the Middle East." *Middle East Studies Association Bulletin* 20 (1, July): 1–12.

Keddie, Nikki R., ed. 1972. *Scholars, Saints, and Sufis: Muslim Religious Institutions in the Middle East*. Berkeley, Calif.: University of California Press.

Knapp, Wilfrid. 1977. *North West Africa: A Political and Economic Survey*. Oxford, UK: Oxford University Press.

Lacouture, Jean, and Simon Lacouture. 1958. *Le Maroc à L'Epreuve*. Paris: Editions du Seuil.

Lahbabi, Mohamed Aziz. 1964. *Le personalisme musulman*. Paris: Presses Universitaires de France.

Landau, Rom. 1962. *Hassan II: King of Morocco*. London: Allen & Unwin.

Lapidus, I. M. 1980. "Islam and the Historical Experience of Muslim Peoples." In Malcolm H. Kerr, ed., *Islamic Studies: A Tradition and Its Problems*. Malibu.

Lapidus, Ira M. 1983. *Contemporary Islamic Movements in Historical Perspective*. Berkeley, Calif.: Institute of International Studies.

Laroui, Abdallah. 1976. *The Crisis of the Arab Intellectual: Traditionalism or Historicism?* Berkeley, Calif.: University of California Press.

———. 1977. *The History of the Maghrib: An Interpretative Essay*. Princeton, N.J.: Princeton University Press.

———. 1980. *Les Origines sociales et culturelles du nationalisme marocain (1830–1912)*. Paris: Maspero.

Laskier, Michael N. 1983. *The Alliance Israelite Universelle and the Jewish Communities of Morocco, 1862–1980*. Albany, N.Y.: State University of New York Press.

Lawless, Richard, and Allan Findlay, eds. 1984. *North Africa: Contemporary Politics and Economic Development*. New York: St. Martin's Press.

Leveau, Remy. 1977. "The Rural Elite as an Element in the Social Stratification of Morocco." In C.A.O. van Nieuwenhuijze, ed., *Commoners, Climbers and Notables*. Leiden: E. J. Brill.

———. 1979. "Réaction de l'Islam Officiel au Renouveau Islamique au Maroc." *L'Annuaire de l'Afrique du Nord* 18:205–218.

———. 1981. "Islam et Contrôle Politique au Maroc." In Ernest Gellner and Jean-Claude Vatin, eds., *Islam et Politique au Maghreb.* Paris: Editions du Centre National de la Recherche Scientifique.

———. 1984. "Aperçu de l'Evolution du Système Politique Marocain depuis Vingt Ans." *Maghreb-Machrek* 106 (October-November-December): 7–36.

———. 1985. *Le Fellah Marocain: Défenseur du Trône,* 2nd ed. Paris: Presses de la Fondation des Sciences Politiques.

———. 1987a. "Pouvoir Politique et Pouvoir Economique dans le Maroc de Hassan II." *Les Cahiers de l'Orient* 6:31–42.

———. 1987b. "Stabilité du pouvoir monarchique et financement de la dette." *Maghreb-Machrek* 118 (October-November-December): 5–19.

Lewis, William H. 1969. "Politics and Islam in North Africa." *Current History* 76 (March): 119–121.

Maher, Vanessa. 1974. *Women and Property in Morocco.* Cambridge, UK: Cambridge University Press.

———. 1978. "Women and Social Change in Morocco." In Lois Beck and Nikki Keddie, eds., *Women in the Muslim World.* Cambridge, Mass.: Harvard University Press.

Mannheim, Karl. 1971. "Conservative Thought." In Kurt H. Wolff, ed., *From Karl Mannheim.* New York: Oxford University Press.

Marais, Octave. 1969. "Les relations entre la monarchie et la classe dirigeante au Maroc." *Revue Française de Science Politique* 19:1172–1186.

———. 1973a. "Elites Intermédiaires, Pouvoir et Légitimité dans le Maroc Indépendant." In Centre de Recherches et d'Etudes sur les Sociétés Méditerranéennes (CRESM), *Elites, Pouvoir et Légitimité au Maghreb.* Paris: Editions du Centre National de la Recherche Scientifique.

———. 1973b. "The Ruling Class in Morocco." In I. William Zartman, ed., *Man, State, and Society in the Contemporary Maghrib.* New York: Praeger.

Marshall, Susan E. 1979. "Islamic Revival in the Maghreb: The Utility of Tradition for Modernizing Elites." *Studies in International Comparative Development* 14 (2, Summer): 95–108.

Masback, Craig. 1986. "The Moroccan Paradox." *The Runner* (August): 28–37, 83.

Mernissi, Fatima. 1975. *Beyond the Veil: Male-Female Dynamics in a Modern Muslim Society.* New York: Schenkman Publishing Co.

———. 1987. *Beyond the Veil.* Revised Edition. Bloomington, Ind.: Indiana University Press.

Micaud, Charles A. 1974. "Bilingualism in North Africa: Cultural and Sociopolitical Implications." *Western Political Quarterly* 27 (1, March): 92–103.

Miller, James A. 1984. *Imlil: A Moroccan Mountain Community in Change.* Boulder, Colo.: Westview Press.

Miller, Judith. July 31, 1986. "Moroccan Jews Talk of the King's Fate, and Theirs." *New York Times.*

Molino, Jean. 1987. "La Culture Comme Enjeu: Considérations Intempestives—Notes Critiques sur la Culture au Maghreb." *L'Annuaire de l'Afrique du Nord.* Paris: CNRS, 29–40.

Montagne, Robert. 1973. *The Berbers: Their Social and Political Organisation.* London: Frank Cass.

Moore, Clement Henry. 1970. *Politics in North Africa: Algeria, Morocco, and Tunisia.* Boston: Little, Brown.

———. 1971. "On Theory and Practice among Arabs." *World Politics* 24 (1, October): 106–126.

Moore, Clement H., and Arlie R. Hochschild. 1968. "Student Unions in North African Politics." *Daedalus* 97 (1, Winter): 21–50.

Moughrabi, Fouad M. 1978. "The Arab Basic Personality: A Critical Survey of the Literature." *International Journal of Middle East Studies* 9:99–112.

Munson, Henry, Jr. 1984. *The House of Si Abd Allah: The Oral History of a Moroccan Family.* New Haven, Conn.: Yale University Press.

———. 1986. "The Social Base of Islamic Militancy in Morocco." *Middle East Journal* 40 (2, Spring): 267–284.

Nedelcovych, Mima Sava. 1980. "Determinants of Political Participation: A Survey Analysis of Moroccan University Students." Ph.D. Thesis. Tallahassee, Fla.: Florida State University.

Nedelcovych, Mima, and Monte Palmer. 1982. "The University and the Radicalization of Disenfranchized Youth: A Case Study of Moroccan University Students." *Journal of South Asian and Middle Eastern Studies* 6 (2, Winter): 21–37.

Nellis, John. 1983. "Tutorial Decentralization in Morocco." *The Journal of Modern African Studies* 21 (3): 483–508.

Nelson, Harold D., ed. 1978. *Morocco: A Country Study,* Washington, D.C.: The American University/U.S. Government Printing Office.

———. 1985. *Morocco: A Country Study,* 5th ed. Washington, D.C.: The American University/U.S. Government Printing Office.

Noin, Daniel. 1970. *La Population Rurale du Maroc.* Paris: Presses Universitaires de France.

Palmer, Monte, and Mima S. Nedelcovych. 1984. "The Political Behavior of Moroccan Students." *Journal of Arab Affairs* 3 (1): 115–131.

Parker, Richard B. 1984. *North Africa: Regional Tensions and Strategic Concerns.* New York: Praeger.

Pascon, Paul, and Mekki Bentahar. 1972. "Ce qui disent 296 jeunes ruraux." In A. Khatibi, ed., *Etudes sociologiques sur le Maroc.* Rabat: Bulletin Economique et Social du Maroc.

Patai, Raphael. 1971. *Society, Culture, and Change in the Middle East,* 3rd enlarged ed. Philadelphia: University of Pennsylvania Press.

––––––. 1976. *The Arab Mind.* New York: Scribner's.

Paul, James A. 1975. "Professionals and Politics in Morocco: A Historical Study of the Mediation of Power and the Creation of Ideology in the Context of European Imperialism." Unpublished Ph.D. dissertation, New York University.

Pye, Lucian W. 1962. *Politics, Personality, and Nation-Building: Burma's Search for Identity.* New Haven, Conn.: Yale University Press.

––––––. 1985. *Asian Power and Politics: The Cultural Dimensions of Authority.* Cambridge, Mass.: The Belknap Press/Harvard University Press.

Quandt, William B. 1969. *Revolution and Political Leadership: Algeria, 1954–1968.* Cambridge, Mass.: The MIT Press.

Rabinow, Paul. 1975. *Symbolic Domination: Cultural Form and Historical Change in Morocco.* Chicago: The University of Chicago Press.

––––––. 1977. *Reflections on Fieldwork in Morocco.* Berkeley, Calif.: University of California Press.

Rassam, Amal. 1980. "Women and Domestic Power in Morocco." *International Journal of Middle East Studies* 12:171–179.

Reginer, J.-J., and J. C. Santucci. 1973. "Armée, Pouvoir et Légitimité au Maroc." In CRESM, *Elites, Pouvoir et Légitimité au Maghreb.* Paris: Editions du Centre National de la Recherche Scientifique.

Rosen, Lawrence. 1972a. "Muslim-Jewish Relations in a Moroccan City." *International Journal of Middle East Studies* 3:435–449.

––––––. 1972b. "The Social and Conceptual Framework of Arab-Berber Relations in Central Morocco." In Ernest Gellner and Charles Micaud, eds., *Arabs and Berbers: From Tribe to Nation in North Africa.* Lexington, Mass.: Lexington Books.

––––––. 1972c. "Rural Political Process and National Political Structure in Morocco." In R. Antoun and I. Harik, eds., *Rural Politics and Social Change in the Middle East.* Bloomington, Ind.: Indiana University Press.

––––––. 1979. "Social Identity and Points of Attachment: Approaches to Social Organization." In Clifford Geertz, Hildred Geertz, and Lawrence Rosen, eds., *Meaning and Order in Moroccan Society:*

Three Essays in Cultural Analysis. Cambridge, UK: Cambridge University Press.

———. 1984. *Bargaining for Reality: The Construction of Social Relations in a Muslim Community*. Chicago: University of Chicago Press.

Rosenbaum, Walter A. 1975. *Political Culture*. New York: Praeger.

Schaar, Stuart. 1973. "King Hassan's Alternatives." In I. William Zartman, ed., *Man, State, and Society in the Contemporary Maghrib*. New York: Praeger.

Schumacher, Edward. October 1, 1984. "Morocco, Where King is King and New Ways New." *New York Times*.

Seddon, David. 1984. "Winter of Discontent: Economic Crisis in Tunisia and Morocco." *MERIP Reports* (October): 7–16.

Sehimi, Mustapha. 1985. "Les élections législatives au Maroc." *Maghreb-Machrek* 107 (January, February, March): 23–51.

———. 1988. "Pleins feux sur les Ministres de Hassan II." *Arabies* 15 (March): 26–33.

Selosse, Jacques. 1973. "Contribution to the Study of Moroccan Attitudes." In I. William Zartman. ed., *Man, State, and Society in the Contemporary Maghrib*. New York: Praeger.

Shils, Edward. 1966. "The Prospect for Lebanese Civility." In Leonard Binder, ed., *Politics in Lebanon*. New York: John Wiley and Sons.

———. 1968. *Political Development in the New States*. The Hague: Mouton.

Shuster, James R. 1973. "Bureaucratic Transition in Morocco." In I. William Zartman, ed., *Man, State, and Society in the Contemporary Maghrib*. New York: Praeger.

Souriau, Christiane. 1983. "Quelques données comparatives sur les institutions islamiques actuelles du Maghreb." In Christiane Souriau, ed., *Le Maghreb musulman en 1979*. Paris: Editions du Centre National de la Recherche Scientifique.

Spencer, William. 1980. *Historical Dictionary of Morocco*. African Historical Dictionaries, 24. Metuchen, N.J.: The Scarecrow Press.

Stone, Russell A. 1973. "Anticipated Mobility to Elite Status Among Middle Eastern University Students." *International Review of History and Political Science* 10 (4): 1–17.

Suleiman, Michael W. 1985. "Socialization to Politics in Morocco: Sex and Regional Factors." *International Journal of Middle East Studies* 17:313–327.

Swearingen, Will D. 1987. *Moroccan Mirages: Agrarian Dreams and Deceptions, 1912–1986*. Princeton, N.J.: Princeton University Press.

Talmon, J. L. 1965. *The Origins of Totalitarian Democracy*. New York: Praeger.

Tessler, Mark A. 1973. "The Tunisians." In Mark A. Tessler, William M. O'Barr, and David H. Spain, eds., *Tradition and Identity in Changing Africa.* New York: Harper and Row.

————. 1976. "Development, Oil, and Change in the Maghreb." In Naihem A. Sherbiny and Mark A. Tessler, eds., *Arab Oil: Impact on the Arab Countries and Global Implications.* New York: Praeger.

————. 1978. "The Identity of Religious Minorities in Non-Secular States: Jews in Tunisia and Morocco and Arabs in Israel." *Comparative Studies in Society and History* 20 (3): 359–373.

————. 1979. "Minorities in Retreat: The Jews of the Maghreb." In R. D. McLaurin, ed., *The Political Role of Minorities in the Middle East.* New York: Praeger.

————. 1982. "Morocco: Institutional Pluralism and Monarchical Dominance." In I. William Zartman and others, *Political Elites in Arab North Africa.* New York: Longman.

————. 1984a. "Continuity and Change in Moroccan Politics. Part 1: Challenge and Response in Hassan's Morocco." *UFSI Reports.* Hanover, N.H.: Universities Field Staff International, Inc.

————. 1984b. "Continuity and Change in Moroccan Politics. Part 2: New Troubles and Deepening Doubts." *UFSI Reports.* Hanover, N.H.: Universities Field Staff International, Inc.

Tessler, Mark A., and others. 1986. *The Evaluation and Application of Survey Research in the Arab World.* Boulder, Colo.: Westview Press.

Tessler, Mark A., and Linda L. Hawkins. 1980. "The Political Culture of Jews in Tunisia and Morocco." *International Journal of Middle East Studies* 11:59–86.

Tessler, Mark A., and John P. Entelis. 1986. "Kingdom of Morocco." In David E. Long and Bernard Reich, eds., *The Government and Politics of the Middle East and North Africa,* 2nd ed. Boulder, Colo.: Westview Press.

Tozy, Mohamed. 1979. "Monopolisation de la Production Symbolique et Hiérarchisation du Champ Politico-Religieux au Maroc." *Annuaire de l'Afrique du Nord* 18:219–234.

————. 1984. "Champ et Contre-Champ Politico-Religieux au Maroc." Thèse pour le Doctorat d'Etat en Science Politique, Aix-Marseille.

Vinogradov, Amal, and John Waterbury. 1971. "Situations of Contested Legitimacy in Morocco: An Alternative Framework." *Comparative Studies in Society and History* 13 (1, January): 32–59.

von Grunebaum, G. E. 1964. *Modern Islam: The Search for Cultural Identity.* New York: Vintage Books.

Waltz, Susan. 1986. "Islamist Appeal in Tunisia." *The Middle East Journal* 40 (4, Autumn): 651–670.

Waterbury, John. 1969. "Kingdom-Building and the Control of the Opposition in Morocco: The Monarchical Uses of Justice." *Government and Opposition* 5 (1, Winter): 41–53.

————. 1970. *The Commander of the Faithful: The Moroccan Political Elite—A Study of Segmented Politics.* New York: Columbia University Press.

————. 1972. *North for the Trade: The Life and Times of a Berber Merchant.* Berkeley, Calif.: University of California Press.

————. 1973a. "Endemic and Planned Corruption in a Monarchical Regime." *World Politics* 25 (4, July): 533–555.

————. 1973b. "Tribalism, Trade and Politics: The Transformation of the Swasa of Morocco." In Ernest Gellner and Charles Micaud, eds., *Arabs and Berbers: From Tribe to Nation in North Africa.* Lexington, Mass.: Lexington Books.

————. 1976. "Corruption, Political Stability and Development: Comparative Evidence from Egypt and Morocco." *Government and Opposition* 11 (Autumn): 426–445.

————. 1979. "La Légitimation du pouvoir au Maghreb: Tradition, Protestation et Répression." In CRESM, *Développements Politiques au Maghreb.* Paris: Centre National de la Recherche Scientifique.

————. November 9, 1982. "Arabs on Edge." *The New York Times.*

————. 1983. *The Egypt of Nasser and Sadat: The Political Economy of Two Regimes.* Princeton, N.J.: Princeton University Press.

Westermarck, Edward. 1926. *Ritual and Belief in Morocco.* 2 vols. London: Macmillan.

Woolman, David S. 1965. *Rebels in the Rif: Abd el Krim and the Rif Rebellion.* London: Oxford University Press.

Worsley, Peter. 1984. *The Three Worlds: Culture and World Development.* Chicago: University of Chicago Press.

Al-Yifrani, Allal. "L'Edition au Maroc: l'edition arabe." *Maghreb-Machrek* 118 (October-November-December): 122–128.

Zartman, I. William. 1964. *Morocco: Problems of New Power.* New York: Atherton Press.

————, ed. 1973. *Man, State, and Society in the Contemporary Maghrib.* New York: Praeger.

————. 1974. "The Study of Elite Circulation." *Comparative Politics* 6 (3, April): 470–485.

————. 1983. "Explaining the Nearly Inexplicable: The Absence of Islam in Moroccan Foreign Policy." In Adeed Dawisha, ed., *Islam in Foreign Policy.* Cambridge, UK: Cambridge University Press.

————. 1985. "Political Dynamics of the Maghrib: The Cultural Dialectic." In Halim Barakat, ed., *Contemporary North Africa: Issues of Development and Integration.* Washington, D.C.: Georgetown University Center for Contemporary Arab Studies.

————. 1987. "King Hassan's New Morocco." In I. William Zartman, ed., *The Political Economy of Morocco.* New York: Praeger Publishers.

Zartman, I. William, and others. 1982. *Political Elites in Arab North Africa.* New York: Longman.

Zonis, Marvin. 1971. *The Political Elite of Iran.* Princeton, N.J.: Princeton University Press.

Index